THE DEPTHS OF GOD

THE DEPTHS OF GOD

Walking Ancient Paths
Into His Presence

For the Spirit searches all things, even the depths of God.
– 1 Corinthians 2:10

BY PAT CHEN

Destiny Image® Publishers, Inc.
P.O. Box 310
Shippensburg, PA 17257-0310

"Speaking to the Purposes of God for This Generation
and for the Generations to Come"

ISBN 0-7684-2191-8
For Worldwide Distribution
Printed in the U.S.A.

This book and all other Destiny Image, Revival Press, MercyPlace,
Fresh Bread, Destiny Image Fiction, and Treasure House books are available
at Christian bookstores and distributors worldwide.

1 2 3 4 5 6 7 8 9 / 09 08 07 06 05 04 03

For a U.S. bookstore nearest you, call
1-800-722-6774.

For more information on foreign distributors, call
717-532-3040.

Or reach us on the Internet:
www.destinyimage.com

DEDICATION

I would like to dedicate this book to my Heavenly Husband, my precious Lord and Savior, Jesus Christ. I would also like to dedicate it to my wonderful earthly husband, Peter. Thank you, Peter, for all of your support and help. I couldn't fulfill God's calling on my life without you.

ACKNOWLEDGMENTS

I have so many good friends and wonderfully supportive brothers and sisters in the Lord. You know who you are. Thank you for helping me to press toward the high calling of Jesus Christ through this book project.

I want to thank Peg de Alminana for being my prayer partner and helping me in the development of this book.

I also want to thank Virene Cardenas for helping me to develop the materials on fasting used in this book.

Thank you intercessors for your dedication to stand before the throne of God in my behalf.

ENDORSEMENTS

There is a cry to the Lord, coming from deep within His Church, for a greater intimacy with Jesus, the Bridegroom of our soul. Within the pages of Pat Chen's book, *Depths of God*, the hungry soul will find nourishing food for the journey into the higher realm of the glory of His Presence! Pat writes from the strength of her own very personal walk with God, as well as from the experience of men and women of God from the pages of Holy Scripture, and from the history of the Church. As we ponder the truths set before us in this most unique and inspiring book, we, too, will experience a holy desperation to enter, more fully, into the *Depths of God*.

—Dotty Schmitt
Immanuel's Church
Author, *The Delight of Being His Daughter*

Pat draws her readers into a secret place of prayer where God can be met like never before. Her discernment of Almighty God and hunger for His direction will ignite your heart to experience dramatic and intense moments that will give a fiery love and consuming passion for God. In her readers, Pat launches a desire to run after God!

—Dr. Cornell (Corkie) Haan
National Facilitator
Mission America Coalition

TABLE OF CONTENTS

Chapter One

STEAL AWAY TO JESUS

How lovely are Thy dwelling places, O Lord of hosts! My soul longed and even yearned for the courts of the Lord.

—Psalm 84:1-2

For five quiet, sacred days my prayer partner and I came apart from the noise and pressures of the world to a cottage nestled in the mountains high above the place where the Russian River meets the Pacific Ocean in northern California. Delighting there in the splendor of that river and the elegance of those gentle, rolling green hills, we became pilgrims, journeying into the depths of God's wonderful presence.

Join our exciting journey as we climb the holy mountain of the Lord, and discover Heaven's secret treasure in your own life.

Come Apart

A vital first key to realizing intimate spiritual desire is coming apart for a season for the sole purpose of seeking God. This means getting away for several days and going to a place where there are no distractions, no pressures, no noise. If you cannot get away for this long, a couple days will do. You must make a spiritual pilgrimage to a place where you can encounter God. Why is it important to get away? You need to find a place where no one can find you but God, a place where you can focus completely on Him. God calls people to come away for a while to rest in Him, but few of us respond to this gentle wooing of the Holy Spirit in our lives. Yet, it is a pivotal key to going deeper in God.

How does one go on such a pilgrimage? You must begin prayerfully, for as you will see, each and every step along the way holds extremely important significance.

Follow the Cloud

Being led by God into the exact place is very important, for this is no vacation or casual retreat. On your prayer journey, you will become like Moses ascending a mountain of prayer to meet God face-to-face. He will meet you there, but first you must permit Him to take you there. Seek Him carefully for the time and the place, and if you will go with a prayer partner, seek His will regarding with whom you will go. Every detail of your prayer pilgrimage is vitally important.

Such a spiritual pilgrimage is not a new idea at all. As a matter of fact, this practice is really very old. The ancient Israelites practiced something similar as recorded in the Book of Numbers.

> *Now on the day that the tabernacle was erected the cloud covered the tabernacle, the tent of the testimony, and in the evening it was like the appearance of fire over the tabernacle, until morning.*
>
> *So it was continuously; the cloud would cover it by day, and the appearance of fire by night. And whenever the cloud was lifted from over the tent, afterward the sons of Israel would then set out; and in the place where the cloud settled down, there the sons of Israel would camp.*
>
> —Numbers 9:15-17

The Bible tells us that the entire nation was led by God's Spirit, either to move forward or to pitch tents and rest. This spiritual journey was comprised of two elements: progress and rest. Both were extremely important to God's purpose in their lives.

In verses 22 and 23, we see that they rested and journeyed at the command of God:

> *Or whether it were two days or a month or a year that the cloud tarried upon the tabernacle, remaining thereon, the children of Israel abode in their tents, and journeyed not: but when it was taken up, they journeyed.*
>
> *At the commandment of the Lord they rested in the tents, and at the commandment of the Lord they journeyed: they kept the charge of the Lord, at the commandment of the Lord by the hand of Moses.*
>
> —Numbers 9:22-23

Your journey in prayer to the depths of God's Spirit is similar to the spiritual journey that the nation of Israel went upon. They journeyed for days at the leading of the Holy Spirit to find the right resting place. It is significant to mention that they were completely led by the Spirit, which was represented in the cloud.

As each of us experiences our own spiritual journey, we also will be led by the Holy Spirit to our own resting places. As you plan your own prayer pilgrimage, commit each and every detail to God. By allowing God to lead you in every detail to that place of rest, you will find His wonderful presence waiting there for you.

A Pilgrim's Way

Not only did the Israelites come apart from their regular routine for times of seeking God, but other biblical characters did so as well. The Bible is replete with examples of prophets and saints who separated themselves for regular seasons of seeking God. For example, Jesus often went away by Himself or took others as prayer partners, such as when Peter, James and John accompanied Him to the Garden of Gethsemane and the Mount of Transfiguration.

Even Jesus saw the need for drawing away from His hectic ministry for times of prayer and rest. The 40 days that Jesus Christ spent in the desert after His baptism serves an example that has been followed by many throughout the centuries and an entire tradition of monasticism was begun by those who sought to free themselves from the daily tug of worldly cares in order to seek intimacy with God.

Although monasticism has been much criticized over the centuries by those who consider it an escape from the world, it nevertheless was rooted in a sincere desire to draw near to God, and was seen for centuries as a key element in the life of total devotion to Jesus Christ.

The early monastics were following the Lord's biblical example: "And when He had sent the multitudes away, He went up on the mountain by Himself to pray. Now when evening came, He was alone there" (Matt. 14:23, NKJV). And Christ commanded His followers to do the same: "Come aside by yourselves to a deserted place and rest a while" (Mark 6:31, NKJV).

Coming apart for times of prayer was also a common practice throughout church history, especially in the early centuries of the Church. Then, it was common for God's people to make pilgrim journeys of prayer and consecration. Madame Jeanne Guyon lived during a time when such seasons of pressing into God's presence, although practiced by only the most devoted believers, were still considered the Christian norm. She said, "We have all been called to the depths of Christ just as surely as we have been called to salvation."[1]

I believe that a closer look at the lives of more modern revivalists such as Finney, Edwards, and others reveals that those who came to know Christ in deeper ways also developed their vast knowledge of Him through this same ancient pathway into His presence.

Coming Apart for Times of Prayer

Times of drawing away from the pressures of crowds and people are vitally important to those seeking to know God and do His will. For our faithfulness in seeking God in solitude, God promises to reward us openly. The Bible says, "But you, when you pray, go into your room, and when you have shut your door, pray to your Father who is in the secret place; and your Father who sees in secret will reward you openly" (Matt. 6:6, NKJV).

The reward of God for drawing away for times of spiritual intimacy, fellowship, and instruction is very real. For example, in the 1700s God rewarded Jonathan Edwards by allowing him to become one of the country's greatest revivalists.

Edwards led one of the early revivals in America, called The Great Awakening. His secret lies in the fact that he was known to spend hours in the woods observing nature and praying. He even built a tree house in the woods where he went to pray with his friends.[2]

Those times of drawing away to be with God were the key to the great empowerment upon his life. Other men and women who experienced God's greatness in powerful ways point to such times of solitude and intimacy as the key to their spiritual reward.

Renowned evangelist Charles Finney claimed that prayer was the secret to great movements of God's Spirit as he would visit cities in the early 1800s. He said, "Unless I had the spirit of prayer I could do nothing. If even for a day or an hour I lost the spirit of grace and supplication, I found myself unable to preach with power and efficiency, or to win souls by personal conversion."[3]

After attending a meeting for young people at a church in Wales, the bookish young evangelist Evan Roberts could no longer concentrate on his studies. He felt drawn to pull away from everything else but prayer. After he drew apart to pray, something amazing began to happen.

"Day and night, without ceasing, he prayed, wept, and sighed for a great spiritual awakening for his beloved Wales. Hours were spent in unbroken, untiring intercession to the chagrin of those who did not understand the symptoms and secret of soul-travail. One thing became clear to him—study was impossible for some unaccountable reason. He had to surrender to this overwhelming, mysterious impulse, surging through his sensitive, awakened soul."[4]

My prayer has been that God would make me as the saints of old and the more recent revivalists, that I might learn God's ways on ancient pathways of prayer and pressing into God. From that holy altar of prayer, I've called on God to fill my heart, mind, and hands with His own words, wisdom, and will.

I encourage you to make this your prayer for your own life as well. And as you choose to make your own pilgrimage of prayer, you will be numbered among a great host of witnesses who have gone before you.

As You Travel

On your holy pilgrimage to the depths of God's presence, you will experience this same leading by God that the ancient Israelites experienced. The Spirit of the Lord will indeed go before you and rest upon you. He will allow you to sense His presence in some wonderful ways as you travel. You may simply feel a special touch from God as you're traveling, or God may give you a word during your Bible study time. You are about to journey into the deep, so come with an expectant heart.

God reveals His presence as you go so that you will know that He is going before you and will meet you there. He also assures you that He is pleased with your desire to know Him better.

Therefore, travel prayerfully. Resist the temptation to turn on the radio to listen to the news report. Even your journey must be dedicated to God. Begin to prayerfully prepare your heart as you work through the various details of your journey.

In our own prayer pilgrimage to the mouth of the Russian River in northern California, my prayer partner and I sensed the presence of God going before us. As we traveled, we were deeply stirred as the Spirit of God descended upon us in the car.

We brushed back holy tears as we passed green pastures in the bloom of early spring along the lovely rolling mountains of northern California. We listened to a CD of John Michael Talbot singing about the Bride. Tenderly, the gentle voice of God showed us that He was taking us by green pastures and still waters to restore our souls. God poured His wonderful presence upon us, and we traveled in silence, filled with peace and expectation about what God had in store.

I'm extremely careful that every step I make is placed in God. I seek Him diligently regarding where to go, with whom to go if I'm not alone, and even what to eat while I'm there.

Some individuals have attempted to go away to meet God in a quiet place and have left frustrated and disappointed. Therefore, be very careful to follow the cloud, which means you must be *led* into that holy place. There is a spiritual world around us that we cannot see. Coming into a place of battle, even if you are not aware of it, can spoil your time with God, leaving you feeling defeated. Let the cloud lead you. Your reward for doing so will be more delightful than you can possibly imagine, and you'll be so glad you did.

Ask God to Take You Deeper

Start by asking God to take you deeper. He is willing to take you there. The Bible says,

And I say to you, ask, and it shall be given to you; seek, and you shall find; knock, and it shall be opened to you.

For everyone who asks, receives; and he who seeks, finds; and to him who knocks, it shall be opened.

Now suppose one of you fathers is asked by his son for a fish; he will not give him a snake instead of a fish, will he?

Or if he is asked for an egg, he will not give him a scorpion, will he?

If you then, being evil, know how to give good gifts to your children, how much more shall your heavenly Father give the Holy Spirit to those who ask Him?

—Luke 11:9-13

Believe it or not, the reason you desire to come into a deeper place in God is because He is drawing you there. The Bible also says, "No one can come to Me, unless the Father who sent Me draws him" (John 6:44). You are responding to the wooing of the Holy Spirit, and He will not disappoint you. You are going to meet Him in a depth that you've never before experienced.

God Will Rise Up

Numbers 10:35 says, "So it was, whenever the ark set out, that Moses said: 'Rise up, O Lord! Let Your enemies be scattered, and let those who hate You flee before You'" (NKJV).

When the Israelites followed the cloud, the heavenly Father manifested His mighty presence before them to conquer their enemies. In similar fashion, as you begin journeying deeper into the Spirit of God in prayer, God's power and strength will become manifested. He will break attacks that have come against you, pull down strongholds, and conquer your enemies.

There, in that blessed place of rest, He will arise, and your enemies will be scattered. God's presence brings power, and even if all the forces of hell have been arrayed against you, hindering you from entering that most holy place, there in that hidden place of refuge you will find Him.

The Beginnings of Months

In the Book of Numbers, we read about a gathering together of God's people called the beginnings of months. This was a special, sacred time set apart by God for His people to seek His face. Without a calendar or planner, God's people were to mark off this regularly scheduled time with a celestial clock. Therefore, each month on the new moon God's people were to come apart to seek Him with all their hearts.

At the beginnings of your months you shall present a burnt offering to the Lord: two young bulls, one ram, and seven lambs in their first year, without blemish...

On the first day you shall have a holy convocation. You shall do no customary work.

—Numbers 28:11,18, NKJV

During this time special sacrifices were offered to God. It was a time of inquiring of the Lord and hearing His voice, of worshipping Him in His house. All work was to cease, for it was a time to rest in God.

Although we are not under the Old Testament laws, their principles remain as beacons of light for us to follow. Jesus Christ quoted from them often and said that He didn't come to abolish these laws but to fulfill them. In other words, these principles now find meaning and expression in our living relationship with Him. Strict guidelines were given, for this time of drawing near to God had to be done in God's way.

God still wants us to set aside time regularly to seek His face, to hear His voice, and to know Him better. Our sacrifices aren't lambs and rams; today we sacrifice our time and effort. Going deeper in God always requires sacrifice. It's a principle that today's Church has lost. We sacrifice time from work, time with our families, money, planning, and much more. We lavish these upon the Lord willingly and joyfully, for nothing is more valuable than knowing Him.

Saints throughout the ages understood the need for sacrifice. It takes time to go beyond the surface.

Why Rest?

As we read in Numbers, the Israelites were not allowed to work during this holy time marked by rest. But why should we rest? In our society, we have little tolerance or understanding of rest. Yet, in God's economy, rest is a pillar.

I always teach my intercessors that when people of prayer lie down, God stands up. Only when our own efforts are at rest can we truly experience how active and powerful God can be on our behalf.

Hebrews 4:1 teaches that rest in God is the promised possession of God's obedient people:

> *Therefore, since a promise remains of entering His rest, let us fear lest any of you seem to have come short of it* (NKJV).

Resting from our activity is vital because it teaches us that we can do nothing of ourselves. We learn that God works in us to do His own good pleasure. Our fleshly activity must cease so that genuine spiritual activity can arise from within us.

In prayer, only God moving in us and upon us can take us into the depths of the Spirit. All the work and effort in the world could never take us there. He must do this work in us as we respond to Him.

An Ancient Love Song

In the Song of Solomon, the Shulamite, who is a picture of the Bride of Christ, is drawn into the depths with her heavenly husband. She sings, "Draw me away! We will run after you" (Song 1:4, NKJV). We, Christ's Bride, call to the depths of His Spirit in similar fashion. We ask Him to draw us deeper, and He delights to do so.

She asks, "Tell me, O you whom I love, where you feed your flock, where you make it rest at noon" (Song 1:7, NKJV). Having asked Him to draw her deeper, she begins to seek a new depth. The Bridegroom responds, telling her how to come deeper (see Song 1:8, NKJV). In other words, He leads Her there, just as He will lead us to that deeper place.

She encounters Him as she enters a new depth, and she hears His voice. She rejoices in the ecstasy of love that she finds in His wonderful presence. Touching her desire, she sings, "He brought me to the banqueting house, and his banner over me was love" (Song 2:4, NKJV).

The Bride sings of her heavenly encounter in the depths of the Spirit when she says, "My beloved spoke, and said to me: 'Rise up, my love, my fair one, and come away'" (Song 2:10, NKJV).

The Shulamite is singing of the encounter that Jesus Christ wants to have with you in the secret places of His presence. Will you respond willingly?

A Sign From Above

In our lovely mountain cottage in northern California, we began our pilgrimage of prayer and immediately sensed the Holy Spirit's touch in increasingly sweet and powerful ways. As we pressed into Christ's presence, His wonderful Spirit descended upon us, lifting us up to new places. A thick blanket of peace covered us as our hearts burned for Him. Crying out with all of our hearts to Him, He came and we were transported.

Words cannot describe the tenderness of His love that flowed freely into our beings, the explosion of His power, the beauty of His peace. To delight in His presence is an unspeakable treasure. Our heart's desire was fulfilled.

As Jesus Christ's holy presence lifted, we stepped outside where we felt lost in a sea of sparkling stars. To our utter delight, the river below us glowed and all the earth was bathed in that moonlit sky. And as if the wonder of it all were not enough, we looked up and realized that the moon was encircled in a giant ring!

It seemed like a sign in the heavens, and God's voice gently, yet powerfully saying, "Yes, My daughters. You have found an ancient path into my presence. Drink deeply of My Spirit, for I have so much more for you."

Does your own heart long for more of God? In the next chapter we will discuss two powerful spiritual companions that will walk with you along the way into depths of His glorious presence. They are holy desperation and spiritual passion.

❧ ENDNOTES ❧

1. Madame Guyon; *Experiencing the Depths of Jesus Christ*; The Seed Sowers; Beaumont, Texas; 1975; copyright by Gene Edwards; p. 1.

2. *America's Great Revivals*; Dimension Books, Bethany Fellowship, Inc.; Minneapolis, Minnesota; reprinted from *Christian Life Magazine*; copyright by *Sunday Magazine*, Inc.; p. 7.

3. Ibid. p. 79.

4. David Matthews; *I Saw the Welsh Revival*; Moody Press; reprinted by End-Time Handmaidens; Jasper, Alaska; p. 10.

Chapter Two

HOLY DESPERATION AND SPIRITUAL PASSION

O God, Thou art my God; I shall seek Thee earnestly; my soul thirsts for Thee, my flesh yearns for Thee, in a dry and weary land where there is no water.

—Psalm 63:1

The Crow's Nest: It was a quaint antique farmhouse cottage nestled into a mountainside with a panoramic view of the Russian River flowing into the Pacific Ocean. A tiny yard wrapped tightly around the steep terrain, and a stone walk that meandered under delightful wisteria bushes laden with purple flowers brought us to a forgotten hand-pumped well.

Because we were carefully placed there by God's own hand, the delightful cottage became a living parable. That forgotten well was to become one of our first lessons.

Interestingly, in the Song of Solomon 4:15, we are called wells. "You are…a well of fresh water." A well is not a stream. Water, which symbolizes the spiritual treasure of the Holy Spirit's presence hidden deep within us, must be *drawn* from a well. Isaiah 12:3 promises: "Therefore you will joyously draw water from the springs of salvation."

But if the depths of God's Spirit lie deep within us, how do we draw it out of the well? Where do we get the right kind of bucket? Jesus had a conversation about this very matter in John 4. This is the story of the woman at the well, who we are told came to draw water and met Jesus. At The Crow's Nest, we came to draw water as well. We were seeking a spiritual experience with the living Lord, so we had much in common with this woman at the well.

To the woman at the well, Jesus said, "Give Me a drink." She replied, "How is it that You, being a Jew, ask me for a drink since I am a Samaritan woman?"

Jesus answered and said to her, "If you knew the gift of God, and who it is who says to you, 'Give Me a drink,' you would have asked Him, and He would have given you living water."

She said to Him, "Sir, You have nothing to draw with, and the well is deep; where then do You get that living water?" (John 4:7-11).

The woman at the well immediately responded with the same question we asked. She wondered how the water—the living water—was to be drawn out of the well. This passage contains a vital key to all spiritual encounters. That key is found in close inspection of Christ's answer.

Jesus answered and said to her, "Everyone who drinks of this water shall thirst again; but whoever drinks of the water that I shall give him shall never thirst…" (John 4:13-14).

The woman asks how to draw living water, and Jesus responds that living water is drawn by means of an individual's thirst. Living water can be drawn from the wells of the Spirit—not with a bucket—but only with the thirst of a human heart. "Blessed is he who hungers and thirsts after righteousness, for he shall be filled" (Matt. 5:6). The extent of your desire for God will determine the extent of your infilling.

Revivalist John G. Lake in his book *Spiritual Hunger,* said this of spiritual desire:

> The hunger of a man's soul must be satisfied. It is a law of God which is in the depths of the Spirit. God will answer the heart that cries. God will answer the soul that asks.[1]

Spiritual hunger or desire is the principle, what Lake calls a spiritual law, which allows us to draw deeply from the Spirit of God. He said, "When the real God-prayer comes into our hearts and the real God-yearning gets hold of our nature, something is going to happen."[2]

Lake believed that it was this principle of spiritual desire that created such a draw upon Heaven that Christ was born into the earth. And again, he says that this same flame of desire will be the spiritual principle that will precede the second coming of Christ. He said:

> The more I study history and prophecy, the more I am convinced that when Jesus Christ was born into the world He was born in answer to a tremendous heart-cry on the part of the world. The world needed God desperately. They wanted a manifestation of God tremendously, and Jesus Christ as Deliverer and Savior came in answer to their soul's cry.
>
> Many look forward to the second coming of Jesus as though mechanically, on a certain date, when certain events come to pass, Jesus is going to appear. I don't see it that way. I believe there must be an overwhelming hunger for the Lord's coming in the hearts of men so that a prayer such as was never prayed in the world before for Christ to come will rise to heaven.[3]

Is this the heart-cry that God is preparing for us today?

Love the Lord With All Your Heart

Holy desperation and spiritual passion fulfill the first commandment to love God with our total heart, our entire being—to let God be the complete and consuming cry of our soul. The heart-cry of which John Lake speaks is all-consuming. It fills your being and overtakes your heart and mind until nothing matters but God. Holy desperation is a cry of the heart that draws so deeply it takes a person's complete strength. The Bible says,

Hear, O Israel: The Lord our God, the Lord is one! You shall love the Lord your God with all your heart, with all your soul, and with all your strength.

—Deuteronomy 6:4-5, NKJV

God showed us how to live a long time ago. When He says, "Hear, O Israel," He's telling us today to listen closely because what He's about to say is extremely important.

When He tells us to love the Lord with all our heart, with all our soul, and with all our might, He's talking about our feelings, our emotions, our mind, our thoughts, our will, and our strength. We are to pursue God with every ounce of strength we have, with every thought, with every resource. We must seek Him with great diligence and with great perseverance.

When we make up our minds that we're going to run after God, then we can be certain that we'll find Him. We'll encounter Him in ways we've never before imagined. The Bible tells us to "draw near to God and He will draw near to you" (Jas. 4:8).

By diligently pursuing God, there will be a giving over of yourself and everything that is within you to Him. As you turn your life over to the Holy Spirit within you, you will find that you connect with a cry. The cry comes from the Spirit of God within you, and you can be sure that such a cry exists and will be released.

When this heart-cry erupts within you, your entire being will be involved. It will take all that is within you—your whole heart, mind, and soul, and it will take all of your strength. At such moments, all that you are and all that is within you reaches for God. You can be sure that He will respond.

Lost in God

There is a place inside of you where you can worship from the very depths of your heart and soul, where your flesh cries out and all your being is consumed in this one pursuit: the pursuit of God.

Once you've entered into this level of prayer, you will discover that it's very natural to worship from this same depth. I call it being lost in God, when you feel that virtually every cell within you is being exerted toward Him. Pressing into God's presence at this depth takes all of your strength—mentally, physically, and spiritually.

There will be times at this depth of God's presence that you will actually feel completely overcome with desire for Him. Once when I was pressing into God at this depth, I had such a hunger and thirst for God that I just felt like I would die if He didn't touch me. The Spirit of God consumed me, and I felt that I wanted Him more than life itself.

It's very difficult to describe, but I felt as though my very life were hanging in the balance except for that touch. When I finally received this divine visitation, I could not help but have the Lord's heart for those who are lost and need to experience Him, too. One turn-of-the-century revivalist named John "Praying" Hyde was known to pray, "Give me souls, lest I die."

Salvation and Evangelism

The apostle Paul well understood this level of holy passion. In Romans, Paul describes his own passion to see his people saved. In Romans 10:1, he said, "Brethren, my heart's desire and my prayer to God for them [the Jews] is for their salvation." Again in Romans 9:1-4, Paul speaks of this great longing. He said, "I am telling the truth in Christ, I am not lying, my conscience bearing me witness in the Holy Spirit, that I have great sorrow and unceasing grief in my heart. For I could wish that I myself were accursed, separated from Christ for the sake of my brethren, my kinsmen according to the flesh, who are Israelites, to whom belongs the adoption as sons and the glory and the covenants and the giving of the Law and the temple service and the promises."

In order to get to this place of passion for souls, you must first have this same passion for Christ in the depths of prayer. Paul had entered into desperation to know Christ. It is this passion for Christ that develops the passion for souls.

Paul said in Philippians 3:7-14:

But whatever things were gain to me, those things I have counted as loss for the sake of Christ.

More than that, I count all things to be loss in view of the surpassing value of knowing Christ Jesus my Lord, for whom I have suffered the loss of all things, and count them but rubbish in order that I may gain Christ, and may be found in Him, not having a righteousness of my own derived from the Law, but that which is through faith in Christ, the righteousness which comes from God on the basis of faith, that I may know Him, and the power of His resurrection and the fellowship of His sufferings, being conformed to His death; in order that I may attain to the resurrection from the dead.

Not that I have already obtained it, or have already become perfect, but I press on in order that I may lay hold of that for which also was laid hold of by Christ Jesus. Brethren, I do not regard myself as having laid hold of it yet; but one thing I do: forgetting what lies behind and reaching forward to what lies ahead, I press on toward the goal for the prize of the upward call of God in Christ Jesus.

Paul was pressing into God. He had a deep level of desperation for Christ, and this passionate relationship with Him created a passion for souls in his inner man. He said, "I count all as loss to gain Christ."

Nevertheless, without maintaining one passion, you cannot obtain the other. It is from an overwhelming passion for God that true passion for souls arises. So, this is how God prepares us to preach the gospel. We get into the prayer closet and this consuming passion for God is converted into a passion for souls. It's then that you can come into the place of saying, "Give me souls, lest I die."

It is this passion for souls birthed in the secret places of consuming prayer that sends out the preacher. We see this in Romans 10:14-15, "How then shall they call on him in whom they have not believed? And how shall they preach unless they are sent?"

Some attempt to develop a passion for souls without nurturing a passion for Christ. Nevertheless, true evangelism is an outflow of this passion for God, which is what I believe happened to Paul. He possessed such a love for his people that he was willing to be accursed if they could be saved. This love and passion for God's people came from taking on God's love and passion for His people in the secret place.

This passion for Jesus brings you into a place of understanding how God feels. It's birthed inside of your being in the secret place of prayer, and it is the key to success in ministry.

Many of us have had it backwards, trying to do the work of evangelism without first gaining a desperation and holy passion for Christ. But with holy desperation, our hearts will be ignited with fiery love for the lost. Salvations that are birthed from this place of intimacy are deep, enduring salvations because they are born in the depths of God's own heart. Such salvations, just as with revivalists like Charles Finney, bring forth converts who are truly, dynamically, radically saved.

In the days of fiery revivalists of the past, these evangelists were known to travel through a town on a train and people in a circumference of 30 miles beyond the train would fall to their knees crying out for salvation. Such phenomenon occurred because of the presence of God that these great men and women carried. It is the fruit of those who have ministered at the altar of holy desperation and spiritual passion.

When our own hearts are aflame with fiery desire for God we reproduce salvations with the same fervency and flame of love for God. In 2 Corinthians 4:5, Paul said, "For we do not preach ourselves but Christ Jesus as Lord, and ourselves as your bond-servants for Jesus' sake."

When our hearts are aflame with God's own fiery passion we transfer our passion for God to those souls to whom we preach. Christ Himself is the One who is preached. I press in to obtain Him, and then I preach Him, and not myself. This is why souls saved under such circumstances are brightly, dynamically, radically saved.

In His face we receive the light of His glory, according to 2 Corinthians 4:6: "For God, who said, 'Light shall shine out of darkness,' is the One who has shone in our hearts to give the light of the knowledge of the glory of God in the face of Christ." That glory shines in our hearts, and we have this light in earthen vessels so that the power is of Him, not of us.

Too often we've preached the power of us, not out of the wealth of Christ in us, which can only be released by touching the depths of God.

Lest I Die

I believe I know exactly what the revivalist John Hyde was feeling when he said, "Give me souls, lest I die." His very life seemed to hang in the balance except for that response from Heaven. As I pressed into God's presence during this time of prayer, everything inside of me ached for Him—every part of my being. I felt as though I was in pain from my head to my toes. I thought, *I just don't know how I can go much longer without You showing up and revealing Yourself to me.* At that moment I literally thought I would die without His deeper touch.

As I continued to pray, I started to feel like giving up, as though I didn't have any more strength to give. I was pressing into God with every ounce of strength within me. At that moment, He showed up. His presence flowed over me in the most wonderful, mighty way. I spent treasured, wonderful moments of divine ecstasy that are beyond earthly description.

At the time, my experience surprised me a little because I didn't know that His presence would come that way. But now I realize that such spiritual exertion is sometimes part of the price we must pay. These experiences can actually be exhausting. There have been times when after such a visitation from God, I would be so spent emotionally, physically and spiritually, that I would need to lie down and rest. I've heard some people say that when you experience the power of the Holy Spirit you're always refreshed afterward. However, sometimes pressing into such a depth can leave you feeling completely drained, albeit at great peace.

Longing to Be Clothed

As we are experiencing such intense spiritual moments, many things happen in us and in the spiritual realm around us. This kind of intensity changes us in dramatic and permanent ways. Let's look further.

For we know that if this earthly tent which is our house is torn down, we have a building from God, a house not made with hands, eternal in the heavens. For indeed in this house we groan, longing to be clothed with our dwelling from heaven; inasmuch as we, having put it on, shall not be found naked. For indeed while we are in this tent, we groan, being burdened, because we do not want to be unclothed, but to be clothed, in order that what is mortal may be swallowed up by life.

—2 Corinthians 5:1-4

I believe that the dwelling from Heaven that this verse speaks of is our spirituality or our spiritual person. I believe in a manner of speaking it's our spiritual body, the ability to walk on this earth as a spiritual being, to exist spirit-to-Spirit with God. This is what we were created for, but we have not been able to walk in this manner since the Fall. On earth we are limited, but the spirit being deep within us longs for the freedom and empowerment that it was created to have with God. I believe that part of what we are longing for is completion in God, becoming whom we were created to be in the realm of the spirit. The apostle John spoke of truth when he said, "Beloved, now we are children of God, and it has not appeared as yet what we shall be. We know that, when He appears, we shall be like Him, because we shall see Him just as He is" (1 John 3:2).

This longing we experience is forming Christ within us. Because the Spirit of God dwells within us, we become a part of the longing that the Holy Spirit has for the Father. Therefore, this longing we experience and express is the deep desire for the consummation of the relationship we have with the Lord.

The Holy Spirit is given to us as the "earnest of our inheritance." Scholars say this means the presence of the Holy Spirit within us is like an engagement ring, revealing the intention of our future wedded state with Jesus Christ.

As His Bride, we are longing for the consummation of our relationship with the Lord, for the time when we will be with Him throughout eternity. Although our eternity with Christ begins at the moment we're saved, our hearts will continue to groan with desire for the fullness of our relationship with Him.

The closer we get to His return, the more our hearts will cry out for our heavenly Bridegroom. Our hearts are longing, yearning for a time to come that our minds do not understand. Our hearts can only find complete rest in Him. "For indeed while we are in this tent, we groan, being burdened, because we do not want to be unclothed, but to be clothed, in order that what is mortal may be swallowed up by life" (2 Cor. 5:4).

A day will come when your mortal man will become immortal. The process was started when you were saved and the Holy Spirit of God took up residence within your heart. A day will come when you will leave this mortal body behind and transcend from this life to the one beyond.

What is divine in you, what is immortal in you is crying out for that heavenly state. Who you really are, the spirit person deep within you, longs for the heavenly realm with a depth of desire that the human heart cannot understand. This very life, this very existence pants for the one beyond. Your heart is longing for a city that your eyes have never seen. Your spiritual feet yearn to walk on golden streets that your earthly mind cannot even imagine.

"Now He who prepared us for this very purpose is God"—the purpose of the mystery of who we are as His Bride is hidden in Him. But in the depths of God within us, we already know what our minds do not know. "For indeed in this house we groan, longing to be cloaked with our dwelling from heaven" (2 Cor. 5:2). That's the ultimate, our final destination: Jesus Christ and our eternal relationship with Him.

"In Him, you also, after listening to the message of truth, the gospel of your salvation—having also believed, you were sealed in Him with the Holy Spirit of promise, who is given as a pledge of our inheritance, with a view to the redemption of God's own possession, to the praise of His glory" (Eph. 1:13-14). These moments of spiritual longing, these moments of divine ecstasy, are that foretaste of glory—that earnest, that deposit that tells us the purpose of our lives lies beyond this earthly realm.

The Holy Spirit was given to us as a pledge or a down payment. In other words, God gave the Holy Spirit to us as a promise, a taste of His glory that shows us that our inheritance is in glory. He allows us to taste what Heaven is like, to know just a little of what we're going to experience for all eternity.

Living With Our Hearts in Heaven

The more we experience these times of heavenly desire, the more our hearts are swept up in God. It's as if our hearts go up in the rapture before the rest of us follows. Increasingly, we experience seasons of longing, seasons when we want nothing more than Him. We don't want Him to do something for us; we don't want Him to fix something or to make something happen.

No, we only want Him. Our highest longing is to be swept up in Him for Himself alone.

Our hearts can lose all interest in this world and even in this life on earth. Paul explains this phenomenon in this way, "We are of good courage, I say, and prefer rather to be absent from the body and to be at home with the Lord" (2 Cor. 5:8). Our purpose for existing is Him—to know Him, to love Him, to long for Him, and to find our soul's completion in Him. Our hearts become consumed by Heaven, and at times we experience what Paul speaks of—this sense that we genuinely prefer to be with Him in Heaven, to be absent from the body and present with the Lord. The more you enter the depths of God, the more you will take on this longing for divine completion.

Paul had one ambition: "Therefore also we have as our ambition, whether at home or absent, to be pleasing to Him" (2 Cor. 5:9). Apart from these experiences in the depths of God you will become motivated by this same driving ambition Paul speaks of. You will want nothing more than to please Him every minute of every day. The thought of grieving Him will become overwhelming, and the longing that you experience deep in your heart will not go away.

Experiencing these things means the Spirit has become large within you, and His sacred trust of pleasing the Father has become your heart's consuming desire.

Positioning Yourself for More of Him

The following is a spiritual exercise I give to intercessors to help them to get into position to obtain more of God. You may find that looking up these verses and praying out their meaning is helpful to your own spiritual journey as you press into greater spiritual passion and holy desperation. Positioning yourself for more of Him is vitally important. Here are some pointers:

✻ *Hunger and thirst*—pray that God will create in you a hunger and thirst for Him. Look up the following Scriptures and pray them aloud: Psalm 63:1-42; Psalm 83:1; Lamentations 2:19.

✻ *Desperation*—pray that God will give you a sense of desperation.

✻ *Helplessness*—pray that God will reveal your need for Him, His purposes in your life and His ways. Look up the following Scriptures and pray them aloud: Psalm 119:107; Psalm 119:130.

✻ Willingness and openness—pray that God will help you to be willing and open to do the following:

> ✻ *Pay the price; sacrifice*—Matthew 16:24-28

> ✻ *Go the distance; be in it for the long haul*—Luke 9:57-62

> ✻ *Wait for Him*—Psalm 37:7-8

> ✻ *Be tried and tested*—Psalm 119:67, 71

> ✻ *To press in; have a passion for possession*—Psalm 63:8

Now that you have entered the depths of God and it has changed you, you will never again be the same!

✑ ENDNOTES ✑

1. John G. Lake, *Spiritual Hunger*, edited by Gordon Lindsay; Christ for the Nations, Inc.; Dallas, Texas; 1987; p. 8.

2. Ibid. p. 7.

3. Ibid. p. 6.

Chapter Three

Searching
the Depths of God

And in the same way the Spirit also helps our weakness; for we do not know how to pray as we should, but the Spirit Himself intercedes for us with groanings too deep for words.

—Romans 8:26

Withdrawing from the ceaseless chatter of worldly noise, which blares through our souls like a cacophony of honking horns and busy traffic, is like climbing a spiritual mountain. It seems fitting that the Lord chose for us The Crow's Nest, neatly nestled atop a mountain overlooking the Sonoma Valley.

The Bible uses the imagery of climbing a mountain to speak of ascending into new places in God. In the same way that we ascend a mountain in the natural using great physical exertion, ascending in the Spirit also exacts a price. Mountain climbing is a progressive journey of steep inclines and broad plateaus. Similarly, climbing to new heights in the Spirit requires a journey.

As we settle in our little cottage, we play gentle, spiritual music that fills the atmosphere with worship. We've spent long hours reading the Word, and after cleaning up from dinner we settle down in the living room to seek God in prayer. Quieting our spirits and focusing on God, it isn't long before the gentle presence of the Holy Spirit descends upon our expectant hearts like a warm blanket.

Silently, we wait before Him. Little noise can be heard except the soft music and an occasional crackling from the fireplace. As the light from the flames dances across the ceiling, our hearts begin to burn with passion for His presence.

A gentle sigh. A quiet calling out, "Oh, Lord!" A whisper, "You're so holy, Lord. You're so holy." Another, "You're so worthy, Father. You're so worthy." Yet another, "I love you with all my heart, oh Lord."

How does one describe the pang of desire that overtakes a human heart? What words can express the longing, the peace, the quiet, the waiting upon a Holy Bridegroom—the expectancy that precedes a visitation of God?

"Breathe upon our waiting hearts, oh Lord."

The quiet whisper of a prayer language. A sigh. An expression of spiritual emotion. Gentle weeping.

As we wait before that flickering fire, blanketed in heavenly peace, our hearts are filling. We are climbing, progressing, ascending the mountain of the Lord. A sense of God's presence charges the atmosphere and grows increasingly real, increasingly manifested. A holy hush. A stillness. An other-worldliness. We're in the same room, and yet we're being transported far from where we started.

Breaking the stillness, a heart cries out in a voice that's barely recognizable for the oil of anointing and the passion of spiritual emotion. Loudly, powerfully one of us groans from the very depths of the Spirit of God. The other joins in.

Every fiber of our being reaches out to God, every atom of our strength. Consumed by His presence, swept up in the Spirit of God, there are no words—only loud, long, sustained cries.

The presence of God bursts forth with each cry, with each spiritual groan. The room is bathed in spiritual light. Our spiritual sensitivity is more alive, more awake than it's ever been, and we discern the very presence of God in our midst. We are overcome by His glory.

Filled with His presence, we rest in what Jeanne Guyon called "mystical sleep." No longer do we perceive time, and even our sense of self has been largely diminished by our sense of Him. Bathed in His glory, we rest in His love—a love that has become a tangible reality overshadowing our perception of anything else. It's a love that comforts, heals, restores, and continues to consume us.

Madame Guyon said this about mystical sleep: "A young bride who has fainted into the embrace of her husband is closely united with him, but she does not enjoy the blessedness of her union with him because she is unconscious. Nonetheless, her husband holds her in his arms while she is in a state of fainting that has come from excess of love. He recalls her to life again tenderly by his caresses, and as she comes to consciousness she knows that she possesses him whom her soul loves and that she is possessed by him. So, too, it is with the believer."[1]

Indiscernibly at first the cloud of glory gently lifts and we become more aware of our surroundings. We have no desire to speak or move; our thoughts seem frozen, halted, and all we sense is a heavy peace that, as with the apostles on the day of Pentecost, causes drunken movements and slurred speech.

We have just climbed a spiritual mountain and touched God. We'll never be the same, for we know that touching His glorious presence has birthed a greater sense of all that He is within us.

Weeping with gratitude, all we can do is thank Him. Love for Him is all we feel, all we know at this moment. It fills our hearts and overwhelms our senses. We love Him completely, wholly, without reservation or halt. We stare into the glowing embers of a dying flame, and we rest in His love.

Searching the Depths of God

Things which eye has not seen and ear has not heard, and which have not entered the heart of man, all that God has prepared for those who love him.

For to us God revealed them through the Spirit; for the Spirit search-
es all things, even the depths of God. For who among men knows the
thoughts of a man except the spirit of the man, which is in Him? Even so
the thoughts of God no one knows except the Spirit of God.

Now we have received, not the spirit of the world, but the Spirit who
is from God, that we might know the things freely given to us by God.

—Corinthians 2:9-12

It is only by allowing the Holy Spirit to take us into the very depths of God that we can begin to know the things that are freely given to us by God. What are these things that can only be discovered in the depths of God's own wonderful heart? "Things which eye has not seen and ear has not heard," things that are hidden and mysterious.

When we search the depths of God, what is revealed to us is beyond the understanding of the rulers of this world, for the Word of God declares it as "the wisdom which none of the rulers of this age has understood" (1 Cor. 2:8).

In the depths of God we discover His glorious purposes for us that we were predestined to walk in before the foundation of the earth, "the hidden wisdom, which God predestined before the ages to our glory" (1 Cor. 2:7). We speak out that wisdom aloud, as our tongue becomes like the pen of a ready writer (see Ps. 45:1).

In 1 Corinthians 2, Paul tells us that he has relied upon the Holy Spirit to lead him into the depths of the Spirit of God. As the Holy Spirit led Paul into the depths of God, we are assured that He will also lead us into those same depths of the Spirit. The very same Spirit that lived in Paul resides in us too and will lead us there as well.

Paul reassures us that we have not received the spirit of the world but the Spirit who is from God. Although we are promised many things because of the gift of the Holy Spirit, few of us number this promise among them: that we might know the things freely given to us by God.

One of the reasons God has given the Holy Spirit to us is so that we will begin to understand the divine purposes of God in our lives; not only for this life, but also the magnificent and glorious purposes planned for us in the life to come. Even though those purposes lie beyond the veil of this life, the Holy Spirit, given to us as a foretaste of eternity, will reveal that divine place to us.

There are many believers who will never reach beyond the veil of this life in their walk with God because they attempt to know Him only through the mind. These passages of Scripture assure us that the mind can never show us this realm of our existence. We were planned for this realm before the earth was created, and it was planned for us. It is a part of our wonderful inheritance in Christ. We are spiritual beings in Him. But the foretaste of God's promise for our lives in Him rests not in the powers of our earthbound minds, souls, and emotions; the foretaste of God in the Holy Spirit lies in the Spirit residing within us. Only He can reveal to us the things that God has given to us.

Paul assures us that we cannot take the journey into the depths of God with the power of the mind. He says, "But a natural man does not accept the things of the Spirit of God; for they are foolishness to him, and he cannot understand them, because they are spiritually appraised" (1 Cor. 2:14).

Does that mean that we are shut out of this revelation of the Spirit? Are the mysteries that God has prepared for us hidden from our sight until after we die and go to glory? Will we have to live this life simply wondering about the glorious realm of God that is our inheritance in Christ Jesus? Absolutely not! For Paul tells us how it is that we have ready access into the divine realm of God through the Holy Spirit—to things which eye has not seen and ear has not heard, neither have they entered into the heart of man. Those mysterious wonders that God has prepared for those who love Him are readily available to us right now in this life through the Holy Spirit.

Paul promises that these mysterious spiritual wonders are revealed to us through the Holy Spirit who resides within us. Though spiritual treasures that eye has not seen are hidden from the natural man, satan, and every other worldly power, they are not hidden from us. These mysteries of God's Spirit, His divine purpose and plan for us that was set in place before He created the earth, are not hidden from us. They are readily revealed through the Holy Spirit: "For to us God revealed them through the Spirit; for the Spirit searches all things, even the depths of God. We have received...the Spirit who is from God, that we might know the things freely given to us by God" (see 1 Cor. 2:10,12).

We are given the ability through the power of the Holy Spirit to look into incredible, glorious mysteries that no one else can know. The depths of God are not blocked or locked. There's no detour sign on the road. There's not even a wait-until-eternity sign posted. The depths of God are a part of our inheritance in God, a part of the foretaste of glory provided to us on this earth as the Bride of Christ.

We can experience Heaven, its glory, power, wisdom, and privilege right here, right now. But we can't have them through the power of the mind and the soul. That's where so many of us find ourselves locked out and tell ourselves that we'll have to wait until glory. Our problem is that we try to get there taking the wrong road. All of the intellectual prowess in the world can never take you into the depths of God's presence. Yet, the simplest child can easily enter.

Madam Jeanne Guyon said, "There is only one requirement, though, that you must follow at all times. It will not interfere with your outward actions, and it may be practiced by princes, kings, priests, soldiers, children, and laborers. This simple requirement is *you must learn to pray from your heart and not your head.* I have found it easy to obtain the presence of God. He desires to be more present to us than we are to seek Him. He desires to give Himself to us far more readily than we are to receive Him. We only need to know *how* to seek God, and this is easier and more natural than breathing."[2]

A Free Gift

The depths of God are freely given to us, and He longs that we might know Him there. He calls us from the depths to the depths that we might know Him. The bride is called in the Song of Solomon into the depths of Christ. "Drink and imbibe deeply, O lovers" (Song 5:1). The inner witness of the Spirit assures us that all who are thirsty may come (see Isa. 55:1).

Although the depths of God are freely given to us, we don't come into the Kingdom of God knowing what they are or experiencing them—even though we already have them. Hence, we must search them out by allowing the Holy Spirit to lead us there. The depths of God are a deep well within our beings from which we must draw, and it is also a stream that flows from within. "You are a garden spring, a well of fresh water, and streams flowing from Lebanon," says the heavenly Bridegroom to His Bride (see Song 4:15).

The apostle Paul goes on to say, "For who has known the mind of the Lord, that he should instruct Him? But we have the mind of Christ" (1 Cor. 2:16).

Searching the depths of God can be likened to the analogy that people used to share about receiving the baptism of the Holy Spirit. It is a gift that you must continue to unwrap so that you can fully understand and experience it. When you receive the Holy Spirit, you must be aware that there is always more, there is always a greater depth.

Unexpectedly, there is another gift to be opened inside of the gift you received. Have you ever received a present wrapped in a big box and you had to keep unwrapping box after box until you got down to the diamond earrings or pearls hidden deep inside a tiny little box? That's what discovering the Holy Spirit within you can be like. There's always more, and the farther you search the greater the treasure.

A Passage Beyond

When we begin to visit the deeper levels of the Spirit of God through prayer, it may not be long before we discover that a deep guttural sound of groaning will erupt from inside our being.

Our passage into the depths of God is marked by a principle well known to New Testament saints and to those revivalists and prayer warriors of recent history who experienced great outpourings of the Holy Spirit. Nevertheless, it's a principle of which many of today's believers are often unaware. The principle is called, for lack of a better term, spiritual groaning.

The Bible says:

For indeed in this house we groan...

—1 Corinthians 5:2

This groaning of our souls is a passage similar to speaking in tongues that gives strength to the new man in Christ within us. Many of us have had the experience of praying so fervently that human words seemed to lose their ability to convey the spiritual reality within us. It was as if we were climbing a mountain in the Spirit, and mere words no longer had the power to move us forward. At such a point of prayer, many have burst into a prayer language. The apostle Paul declared, "...I shall pray with the spirit and I shall pray with the mind also" (1 Cor. 14:15).

Praying in the Spirit can involve a kind of progression. We start out praying about our burdens and concerns. We may have a list of names that we call out before the throne room of Heaven. We speak to God as the Holy Spirit moves upon our hearts, filling our minds with thoughts and words that we then express to Him in prayer. At some point, many people of prayer begin to discover that they enter a kind of plateau. They feel limited in their ability to press into the Spirit of God to the full extent of their spiritual desire.

It's at this point, as we mentioned, that some of us have burst forth in a heavenly language called tongues. To learn more about this powerful experience, see my book, *Intimacy With the Beloved*. As a result, we seem liberated to pray in the Spirit, and our spiritual prayer may be marked by praying in tongues. However, if we continue to press into the Spirit of God using the enablement He has provided for the journey, we may come to another prayer experience.

Just as human words become a plateau from which our spirit man cannot continue to ascend without special enabling from the Holy Spirit, going even deeper may require yet another experience.

Before that occurs, you may experience many types of tongues and many different prayer languages. One minute your tongues seem to be imploring God in supplication; at another time your tongues are bold and loud and directed right at the enemy as if in warfare. At one moment your tongues seem simple and repetitive, and at another they seem sophisticated and intricate. You may even receive several new prayer languages that are distinctly different from each other as you continue to unwrap this gift of prayer. That's why I've been known to call the gift of tongues "the language of love and war."

As you seek to press beyond this depth, you may experience the eruption of even another spiritual gift from the Spirit of God—spiritual groaning.

Think of it like a rocket. You might consider that natural language is the first stage that falls off in your journey into the depths of God. The gift of tongues is the second, and the third level of spiritual empowerment is groanings.

Groanings, tongues, weeping in the Spirit and so many other spiritual expressions form a kind of language of the Spirit and a type of intercession. No one knows why God chose these sounds to express such depth and drama in the spiritual realm, but He did.

These sounds bring pleasure to Him and He responds dramatically to them when they are truly from the Holy Spirit. They form a kind of wooing of the Spirit that draws God to us. We are responding to His wooing, and then we are wooing Him back in the heavenly drama of divine romance. At the same time, we are interceding on behalf of others.

The Spirit of God searches the depths of God. "Likewise the Spirit also helps in our weaknesses. For we do not know what we should pray for as we ought, but the Spirit Himself makes intercession for us with groanings which cannot be uttered. Now He who searches the heart knows what the mind of the Spirit is, because He makes intercession for the saints according to the will of God" (Rom. 8:26-27, NKJV).

Only the Holy Spirit can take you into the depths of God, as this passage reveals, and He does that through spiritual groanings. These groanings are one of the most powerful keys of going deeper in God. Let's examine this powerful Holy Spirit booster rocket that seems to propel us forward into the very depths of God's Spirit.

Longing to be Clothed

For we know that if the earthly tent which is our house is torn down, we have a building from God, a house not made with hands, eternal in the heavens. For indeed in this house we groan, longing to be clothed with our dwelling from heaven.

—2 Corinthians 5:1-2

The Bible provides a remarkable reason for spiritual groanings: We groan in the Spirit when we pray because we long to be clothed with our dwelling from Heaven, and we do no want to be found naked. What does this mean? What is our dwelling from Heaven? And why does not having this dwelling from Heaven cause us to be naked? What do we need to be clothed with, and what would cause us to be found naked?

To answer these questions, let's look at some instances where the Bible warns us not to be found naked. In Revelation 3:17, Christ warns the Laodicean church about the need to be clothed and not found naked:

> *Because you say, "I am rich, and have become wealthy, and have need of nothing," and you do not know that you are wretched and miserable and poor and blind and naked, I advise you to buy from Me gold refined by fire, that you may become rich, and white garments, that you may clothe yourself, and that the shame of your nakedness may not be revealed; and eye salve to anoint your eyes, that you may see."*
>
> —Revelation 3:17-18

Here the nakedness is their lack of spirituality, their lack of spiritual depth and understanding. They are naked but don't realize how spiritually shallow they really are. The Laodiceans are looking at the outward things they've accomplished for God and are forgetting that "the Lord looks at the heart" (1 Sam. 16:7, NKJV).

The Lord encourages the Laodiceans to obtain white garments from Him, clothing that will keep them from being found naked. Could it be that this clothing is similar to what Paul was speaking of in Second Corinthians?

Another passage in Revelation warns against nakedness: "Behold, I am coming like a thief. Blessed is the one who stays awake and keeps his garments, lest he walk about naked and men see his shame" (Rev. 16:15). Here again the Lord warns us against the shame of nakedness. But what is being put on or not put on is not physical clothing. Rather, it is a spiritual covering that believers are expected to wear, a covering that can only be seen by those with spiritual vision, else the Laodiceans would have realized their lack.

The lack of an invisible spiritual covering of garments presents a great problem to one who attends the marriage supper of the Lamb and is, as Paul would have said, "found naked" or found without the right clothing.

But when the king came in to look over the dinner guests, he saw there a man not dressed in wedding clothes, and he said to him, "Friend, how did you come in here without wedding clothes?" And he was speechless.

—Matthew 22:11-12

The wedding garments that this poor soul lacked are clearly described in Revelation 19:7-8. It says, "Let us rejoice and be glad and give the glory to Him, for the marriage of the Lamb has come and His bride has made herself ready. And it was given to her to clothe herself in fine linen, bright and clean; for the fine linen is the righteous acts of the saints."

This is the same wedding garment that must be found without "spot or wrinkle," (see Eph. 5:27) and "spotless and blameless" (see 2 Pet. 3:14).

I'm convinced that the dwelling from Heaven that the apostle Paul is teaching us about is our spirituality. It's a spirituality that is demonstrated in pure, righteous acts, but is called a garment, clothing, or a tent or tabernacle by Paul. I believe that if we could see with heavenly vision, we would see a white covering of light surrounding those saints who walk in the light with Jesus Christ. The covering, although invisible to the natural senses, is as real and tangible as any object on the earth.

It's this garment, this covering that is dramatically affected when we press into the depths of God's presence through the groanings of the Holy Spirit. Who we are, our righteous walk, our wisdom and our holiness in God is dramatically matured as we labor in this place of prayer, while continuing to read and obey His mighty Word.

When we touch God at this depth of the Holy Spirit, we are changed into His likeness. "But we all, with unveiled face beholding as in a mirror the glory of the Lord, are being transformed into the same image from glory to glory, just as from the Lord, the Spirit" (2 Cor. 3:18).

Walking With God in the Cool of the Day

Adam and Eve were more than physical beings. They were spiritual beings as well, and God walked with them. Genesis 3:8 reads, "And they heard the sound of the Lord God walking in the garden in the cool of the day." They walked with God in the most practical and spiritual sense.

I believe that this spiritual clothing Paul speaks about was what clothed Adam and Eve. For as you recall, until they sinned they were clothed with God's glory alone, and not with physical clothes. When that glory left after their sin, they hid for the shame of their nakedness. At that moment, as Paul says, they started longing to be clothed once again.

To me, it's as though Paul is saying we're limited on this earth right now, yet our inner spirit man longs for that freedom that we had from the very start, when mankind was created at the very beginning of time.

We are longing to reclaim the fullness of that relationship with God, to walk once again with God in the cool of the day. Our hearts groan for the consummation of our relationship with the Lord because deep down we know we were created for much more. In addition to that, the Holy Spirit inside of our hearts longs for the time when we will be with Him eternally. Yes, we are saved and eternity has begun deep inside our hearts, but there is a greater, more glorious life with God to come that our spirits long for and groan for until we are with Him.

Prepared for This Purpose

For indeed while we are in this tent, we groan, being burdened, because we do not want to be unclothed but to be clothed, in order that what is mortal may be swallowed up by life. Now he who prepared us for this very purpose is God.

—2 Corinthians 5:4-5

God prepared us for this very purpose. For indeed in this house we groan, longing to be clothed with our dwelling from Heaven. God has literally prepared us for the very purpose of longing to be with Him, of finding our completion in Him in eternity.

This desire becomes so consuming during times of intimate fellowship with God that it crosses over into groaning, which becomes the only way to express it. Just as prayer crosses over into tongues, your desire crosses over into groaning. When you are consumed with longing for Him, the groanings are words that God understands. He understands and responds to these utterings.

Groanings Bring Forth the Eternal

Groanings bring forth the eternal things planned from the beginning of time in order to bring forth the completion of them at the end of time:

The Lord will go forth like a warrior, He will arouse His zeal like a man of war. He will utter a shout, yes, He will raise a war cry. He will prevail against His enemies. "I have kept silent for a long time, I have kept still and restrained Myself. Now like a woman in labor I will groan, I will both gasp and pant.

—Isaiah 42:13-14

Groaning, travail, and labor bring deliverance, energy, power, passion, and growth; and they accomplish the eternal work and purposes of God. Groanings bring forth new things and breakthroughs in prayer, for Isaiah 42:8-9 says,

I am the Lord, that is My name; I will not give My glory to another, nor My praise to graven images. Behold, the former things have come to pass, now I declare new things; before they spring forth I proclaim them to you.

History books that record the events surrounding the revivals of the Holy Spirit in the early 1900s remark on the place of groaning and soul travail in the witnessing of Holy Spirit outpourings. The book *The Great Revival in Wales* records: "Deep, spiritual revivals come through soul-travail. 'For as soon as Zion travailed, she brought forth her children' (Isa. 66:8). All successful revivalists and great soul-winners bear testimony to the necessity of soul-travail as condition of success."[3]

Again we read, "No words can depict the awfulness of Evan Roberts' agony, they say. He clutched the Bible nervously, turned over its pages hurriedly, and then suddenly his face became distorted with pain...Oh! oh! oh! repeated over and over again in varied tones, were heart-piercing in the extreme. He himself believes that it is by such an ordeal that God enables him to agonize for souls.

"But others who are familiar with the experiences of David Brainerd and other saintly revivalists of former days, and who know how day by day this young man in private as well as in public lives in fellowship with God that is intimate and deep, interpret such an incident in the light of those words, 'Ye shall indeed drink My cup and be baptized with the baptism that I am baptized with.'"[4]

Deliverance Through Groaning

Right now the flesh is a kind of bondage, and the entire creation is in bondage under the principle of sin. In this light, groanings become a cry for release from bondage.

We are groaning and actually pressing in to know Him, but we are also being delivered from our own bondage at the same time. We are also being used by the Holy Spirit in intercession to bring deliverance to the world and others, for God hears our groanings. The Bible states: "For He looked down from His holy height; from heaven the Lord gazed upon the earth, to hear the groaning of the prisoner; to set free those who were doomed to death." (Ps. 102:19-20).

Groanings are linked to freeing those who are imprisoned, and when these cries come before the throne of glory, we can be sure that God hears them. Groaning affects the individual and influences world history, hastening the return of the Lord. He will move Heaven and earth to respond to His Bride. Sometimes that prison involves our spirits being bound to the flesh and needing to be released into the blessed liberty of the Spirit. Sometimes the prison is the snare of circumstance and the trap of the enemy of our souls.

"Blessed be the Lord, who daily bears our burden, the God who is our salvation. God is to us a God of deliverances," according to Psalm 68:19-20. He is our Savior every day of our lives, and He is continuing to save us from this dark world. Sadly, like the church of Laodicea, we often are too blind to realize how much we need His deliverance. Joyfully, the Holy Spirit within knows it very well.

The groaning of the prisoner was the sound from God's people that preceded their deliverance from Egypt. The Bible speaks of this groaning in Exodus 2:23-24: "And the sons of Israel sighed because of the bondage, and they cried out; and their cry for help because of their bondage rose up to God. So God heard their groaning; and God remembered His covenant with Abraham, Isaac, and Jacob." It was this spiritual groaning that moved the hand of God into action on behalf of the children of Israel.

Again, in Exodus 6:5 God tells us that groaning was a sound that moved Him: "And furthermore I have heard the groaning of the sons of Israel, because the Egyptians are holding them in bondage; and I have remembered My covenant."

Delivered From the Bondage of the Flesh and World

In this same way, God will deliver His people from the world and the power of satan. Egypt in the Scriptures represents the world held captive under the power of satan, its pharaoh. We can be certain that God will respond to the groanings of our spirits in the same manner as He did with Egypt and the

Israelites. God judged the idols that Egypt worshipped—frogs, cattle, the Nile River, mankind—in order to deliver His people out of their power. When our spirits cry out to God in groanings, God will be stirred to do no less on our behalf.

According to the Bible, the entire world is enslaved in a principle of bondage:

> *For the anxious longing of the creation waits eagerly for the revealing of the sons of God. For the creation was subjected to futility, not of its own will, but because of Him who subjected it, in hope that the creation itself also will be set free from its slavery to corruption into the freedom of the glory of the children of God. For we know that the whole creation groans and suffers the pains of childbirth together until now. And not only this, but also we ourselves, having the first fruits of the Spirit, even we ourselves groan within ourselves, waiting eagerly for our adoption as sons, the redemption of our body.*
>
> —Romans 8:19-23

There is a principle of death and bondage that lies over the entire creation. It is against this bondage that our spirits cry out in groanings to God. I believe that the deliverance from Egypt was a type or shadow of what is to come in the earth. When God's people groan under the bondage of death and satan, God hears them and begins moving mightily to pull down the idols that hold them captive. Although we may not realize it, groaning in the Spirit of God is a key to deliverance.

The earth actually longs for the sons of God to be revealed to the earth. All Heaven, all nature, and all the earth are in agreement with God that we will come to the fullness of our calling and destination. We will become the witness of God in the earth, in order to glorify Him.

The whole earth groans and travails awaiting the purposes of God to be totally fulfilled. The Bible promises that the creation will be set free from its slavery. Creation waits together with us for something glorious and wonderful to happen, something beyond anything our hearts could imagine. We are all awaiting the completion of events that began at the Cross of Christ where His precious blood was shed for all mankind.

This groaning is similar to childbirth: "For we know that the whole creation groans and suffers the pains of childbirth together until now." All of creation, the whole creation groans and suffers the pains of childbirth. We ourselves groan within ourselves, waiting eagerly for our adoption as sons, the redemption of our body. Our groaning is touching the creative purposes that God has in the earth. Our groaning is touching the glorious plan of completion and redemption of all things at Christ's coming. We groan because our spirits know very well that a day is coming when they will find completion and perfect union in God. We groan as we await that day, and our groans actually reach into the purposes of God and speed up the process.

For in hope we have been saved, but hope that is seen is not hope; but why does one also hope for what he sees? But if we hope for what we do not see, with perseverance we wait eagerly for it.

—Romans 8:24-25

This scripture reveals that although we are living this life, we are also on a journey. We live a temporal life in a temporal place, yet at the same time we are on an eternal journey with an eternal purpose.

Touching Our Creative Purpose

The Bible links God's creative purpose in our lives with groanings that help bring that creative purpose forth. This moving of the Holy Spirit in the depths of prayer helps us to become like Christ. Romans 8:29 says, "For whom He foreknew, He also predestined to become conformed to the image of His Son." That person God foreknew was a totally redeemed person, adopted as

God's Son. The groanings of the Spirit within recall that person foreknown of God, according to Romans 8:23. "We ourselves, having the first fruits of the Spirit, even we ourselves groan within ourselves, waiting eagerly for our adoption as sons, the redemption of our body." This groaning within ourselves is one part of the process that births the person who is conformed into the image of Christ.

We are too weak to cause this new man to come forth in resurrected power, but the Spirit of God within us is not. "And in the same way the Spirit also helps our weakness; for we do not know how to pray as we should, but the Spirit Himself intercedes for us with groanings too deep for words" (Rom. 8:26).

Only the Holy Spirit Himself can visit this depth of God that is too deep for human words. Here, He is able to bring forth this birthing of the new man within our beings, with righteous clothing that will allow us to stand before Christ spotless and without wrinkle.

Another level of the new man in Christ comes forth by groaning. Not only is a mature person being formed, but there is also a communion, a relationship that transpires at a deeper level, as if two separated lovers, longing for one another, are finally united. Touching God at this depth of the Spirit causes a birthing to come forth—a birthing of God's purposes, His presence, His life, and His plans.

The earth is in agreement with God to see the sons of God. When His people come to the fullness of their calling and destiny, when they touch the reason that they were formed, the earth will be released into its destiny too. It longs to see God's image reflected in man on this earth.

A Fountain of Healing

Groanings of the Holy Spirit will precede Christ's return and they will increase as that time draws near and end-time, world, or global events unfold or are revealed, according to Zechariah 12:11-12;13:1: "In that day there will be a great mourning in Jerusalem, like the mourning of Hadadrimmon in the plain of Megiddo. And the land will mourn, every family by itself... In that day a fountain will be opened for the house of David and for the inhabitants of Jerusalem." A fountain of cleansing, healing, and salvation will be opened up in Jerusalem because God will hear and respond to the groaning of His people in bondage once more.

✤ ENDNOTES ✤

1. Madame Guyon; *Union with God;* The Seed Sowers; Sargent, Georgia; 1999; copyright by Gene Edwards; p. 36.

2. Madam Guyon; Donna C. Authur, Editor; *Experiencing God through Prayer;* Whitaker House; 1984; Springdale, Pennsylvania; p. 13.

3. Solomon Benjamin; *The Great Revival in Wales;* 1905; S.B. Shaw; Chicago, IL; p. 173.

4. Ibid. p. 174.

Chapter Four

SEEKING HIM
THROUGH FASTING

Then your light will break out like the dawn, and your recovery will speedily spring forth; and your righteousness will go before you; the glory of the Lord will be your rear guard.

—Isaiah 58:8

Our spiritual pilgrimage was very well planned, with every detail bathed in prayer and careful consideration. Believe it or not, one of the most important details was what we would eat or not eat.

After much discussion, we determined that a Daniel fast of sorts was what God was leading us into. When you have a prayer partner, it often works best to eat simply but not attempt a total fast. We would eat no meat, pastries or desserts, and no rich or spicy foods. Instead, we would eat lots of fresh fruits and vegetables prepared fresh or lightly steamed, healthy cheeses, organic whole grains cooked very plainly, nuts and dried fruits, soymilk, teas, and juices.

Shopping in preparation for our weeklong prayer journey proved to be its own adventure. Northern California offers some of the best selections of healthy foods in the country. So, we visited one of the most popular health-food grocers in the region and carted up and down the aisles searching a broad sampling of healthy rolled oats and balsamic rice; freshly baked twelve-grain, pumpernickel, and other wonderful whole grain breads; aromatic, smoked, and aged cheddar, Swiss and goat cheeses; a wide variety of exotic juices and whole grain pastas; organic fruits and vegetables of every size and description—more wonderful, healthy choices than you could ever sample.

We thought through and discussed many food selection issues, such as how to get enough protein and should we eliminate caffeine. Determining that our selections would not only nourish our bodies adequately, but would also provide a degree of physical detoxification, we packed our car with delicious fresh fruits and vegetables and started on our exciting prayer adventure.

Why So Much Interest?

Why so much interest and careful planning about food? When committing a week or several days to seeking the Lord in prayer, fasting even partially can offer an enormous benefit of spiritual empowerment. Some may decide to abstain completely from food altogether, although doing so may or may not be God's best for you.

Remember, you do not want to lose the prayer focus of your pilgrimage. If totally abstaining from food will cause you to spend the week thinking and talking about what you're not eating, then it's best to limit what you intend to eat in a predetermined way.

Because I had a prayer partner and we planned to use the week journaling and writing as well as praying, we decided that our best fasting plan was a modified Daniel fast. When I've gone alone on a personal prayer retreat, I have fasted with water only or bread and water and juices.

Here's one word of caution: the one thing you never want to do is have no eating plan. Don't lose the precious treasure of this spiritual experience by spending it snacking and gossiping and otherwise feeding the flesh. This is a spiritual journey. If you need a vacation, then take one. But don't get the two purposes confused and miss out on one of the most blessed and precious spiritual experiences of your life.

Because what you choose to eat or not eat can make or break this powerful experience, I've decided to commit an entire chapter to fasting and its role in seasons of intense, intimate prayer and communication or communion with God. Fasting is very biblical, and it has many powerful benefits to help you draw near to God.

Discovering the Power and Promise of Fasting

We who desire to be a part of the move of God in these closing hours are responding to the call of the Lord to seek Him and to know His heart through intimate fellowship, earnest prayer, and much fasting. As our hearts are stirred to reach for greater intimacy and deeper fellowship, we embrace the promise of 2 Chronicles 7:14 (NKJV):

> *If My people who are called by My name will humble themselves, and pray and seek My face, and turn from their wicked ways, then I will hear from heaven, and will forgive their sin and heal their land.*

Fasting is a voluntary humbling of our flesh in order to better pursue the things of the Spirit. What does it really mean to fast? *Fasting* means to "abstain from food beyond the usual time." It can imply that we eat very little or nothing.

The word *fast* in the Greek language means hunger. Consider some of the references connected with fasting in the Old Testament, such as "to not eat bread," "to afflict the soul," "to put down the soul," "to humble the soul," "to weaken the soul," "to brow-beat the soul."

The world in which we live can exert a powerful drawing force upon our everyday lives. When we feel our souls being drawn away from God and toward the pleasures and cares of this world, we can return to the Lord very quickly by withdrawing from distractions and denying ourselves physical food for a season as we feed upon His Word. Fasting charges your spirit man and dulls your flesh.

There is nothing more satisfying and energizing to the soul as sweet solitude with Jesus. As you enter that secret place and begin to worship Him and "eat" His Word, allowing His Holy Spirit to remove those things that would hinder His presence, you begin to feel fresh energy flowing in the most inward place of your spirit man. The dryness and hardness that had been settling in your soul begins to soften as the dew of His Word falls easily on the ground of your fasted heart.

Fasting is a wonderful way to answer God's call to "break up your uncultivated ground, for it is time to seek the Lord, to inquire for and of Him, and to require His favor, till He comes and teaches you righteousness and rains His righteous gift of salvation upon you" (Hos. 10:12, AMP).

Hiding Away in Him

In the Scriptures, fasting generally implies abstaining from food, or even from food and water. One of the classic Scriptures we use when studying fasting is Isaiah 58. But my favorite scripture is Job 23:12 (AMP). Let's take a closer look at this passage:

I have not gone back from the commandment of His lips; I have esteemed and treasured the words of His mouth more than my necessary food.

"I have not gone back from the commandment of His lips" means that I have stayed with His words, I have remained faithful to that relationship that comes from an intimacy with Him. The verse continues, "I have esteemed and treasured the words of His mouth." The word *esteemed* means "to put a value on…to prize…to have a high regard for…to have a favorable opinion of something or someone." I have set my value, that which is very important to me, that which I prize, on God. He is more important than my necessary food.

Esteem also means "to respect" and "to revere." When I come before the Lord with fasting I am respecting Jesus Christ, because He is the Word. So, I say, "Jesus, I esteem You—the Word of God—as more necessary, more wonderful, more valuable, more prized that even my necessary food."

When I declare that God is more highly desirable to me than food, the Holy Spirit within me helps me to lose my natural desire for physical food. When the Scripture says, "treasured up," it also means to hide. *Strong's Concordance* says to *hide* means "to hoard, to reserve, and also to keep secret." This Scripture implies that I have hoarded, I have reserved, I have kept secret, I have hidden His Word within my heart. I have kept Jesus in me instead of natural food. I have put Him in me instead of cakes, cookies, chocolate, and coca-colas.

Treasured up also means "to go into a den." That means to go into a nice cozy room, a place where you like to go, curl up, and read a good book. So that's what you do when you fast—you shut yourself in with the Bible. "Thy word have I hid in mine heart, that I might not sin against thee" (Psalm 119:11 KJV). The word *hid* in this verse has the same meaning as *treasured up* in Job 23:12.

When you fast you should not go around with a long drawn face, but instead praise Him with your heart and look as though you are feeling great, not as though your stomach is hurting or growling.

Fasting Tests Our Hearts

Deuteronomy 8:1-2 (NKJV) says:

Every commandment which I command you today you must be careful to observe, that you may live and multiply, and go in and possess the land of which the Lord swore to your fathers. And you shall remember that the Lord your God led you all the way these forty years in the wilderness, to humble you and test you, to know what was in your heart, whether you would keep His commandments or not.

The Lord is always testing us, and He is always looking to see what is in our hearts, but He also wants us to know the condition of our own hearts. When you are in the desert—that place without food and water—the Lord will cause His words to probe and test your heart to show you its condition. As you respond to His Word, as you obey, your heart will become cleaner and cleaner.

Deuteronomy 8:3 (NIV) says:

He humbled you, causing you to hunger and then feeding you with manna, which neither you nor your fathers had known, to teach you that man does not live on bread alone but on every word that comes from the mouth of the Lord.

"He humbled you." When you start to hunger for God, you find yourself being humbled. He humbles you and you humble yourself. You lower yourself, and then you feed yourself on Him.

The Scripture continues in verses 4 and 5:

Your garments did not wear out on you, nor did your foot swell these forty years. You should know in your heart that as a man chastens his son, so the Lord Your God chastens you.

Because God loves us so much, He's been disciplining us! And I thank Him for it. Sometimes I ask the Lord to do whatever it takes to bring me to a place of perfect intimacy and love for Him. But when tests and trials follow I think, "Maybe I should stop praying that!"

The Promised Land

Deuteronomy: 8:6-9 (NIV) says:

Observe the commands of the Lord your God, walking in His ways and revering Him. For the Lord your God is bringing you into a good land— a land with streams and pools of water, with springs flowing in the valleys and hills; a land with wheat and barley, vines and fig trees, pomegranates, olive oil and honey; a land where bread will not be scarce and you will lack nothing; a land where the rocks are iron and you can dig copper out of the hills.

Note that it says, "A land where bread will not be scarce." God likes us to eat! He likes us to enjoy our food, and He likes us to eat until we are full. There is nothing wrong with having pleasure when you eat. Our food is for our nourishment, our appointed portion, our daily bread. But there is a time to put aside food and eat spiritual food—the Word, Jesus Himself!

Lamentations 3:24 shows us that the priests have a special kind of relationship with food, because the Lord is their portion. We who love Him are a kingdom of priests and kings unto our God. Therefore, when we are serving Him, we are priests unto the Most High God. That means we have the Lord as our prescribed portion. You are actually eating the Word, feasting on Jesus. I fast from physical food, and then I begin to taste and see that the Lord is good (see Psalm 34:8).

Just as you enjoy good food, you can also enjoy God!

Be careful that you do not forget the Lord your God, failing to observe his commands, his laws and his decrees that I am giving you this day.

Otherwise, when you eat and are satisfied, when you build fine houses and settle down, and when your herds and flocks grow large and your silver and gold increase and all you have is multiplied, then your heart will become proud and you will forget the Lord your God, who brought you out of Egypt, out of the land of slavery.

—Deuteronomy 8:11-14, NIV

Spiritual Discipline

Fasting shows that you are serious and committed. It reinforces your attitude of repentance and your heartfelt confession to God. As His Bride, we should fast as a part of our spiritual discipline. The way each of us carries out this exercise will be different even as individuals are different. We need to be diligent, though, to seek the Lord regarding His chosen fast for each of us and to be careful to obey His leading.

We can go for periods of time simply enjoying the pleasures of this world. God has given us that privilege. God has given us food to enjoy, homes to enjoy. Such things are gifts from God that represent His love for us. However, when we begin to lose perspective and our priorities get out of whack, we find ourselves forgetting that it was God who prospered us.

Remember, 1 John 2:16 (NIV):

For everything in the world—the cravings of sinful man, the lust of his eyes and the boasting of what he has and does—comes not from the Father but from the world.

Deny those cravings or lusts and replace them with fasting, prayer, and the Word; and soon you will find yourself enjoying the Lord again even more than your necessary food. If you are on a partial fast, replace your cravings and lusts with food that is good and wholesome. You will discover, as David did in Psalm 119:103 (NIV): "How sweet are your words to my taste, sweeter than honey to my mouth!"

Types of Fasting

There are basically three types of fasts. Two are involuntary and one is voluntary.

The first type of involuntary fast is experiencing a lack of appetite resulting from deep emotions. An example of this is found in the Book of Acts where Paul, on a journey to Rome, was shipwrecked. Acts 27:21 (NIV) says:

After the men had gone a long time without food, Paul stood up before them and said: "Men, you should have taken my advice not to sail from Crete; then you would have spared yourselves this damage and loss."

And in Acts 27:33-34 (NIV) we read:

Just before dawn Paul urged them all to eat. "For the last fourteen days,"
he said, "you have been in constant suspense and have gone without
food—you haven't eaten anything. Now I urge you to take some food. You
need it to survive. Not one of you will lose a single hair from his head."
After he said this, he took some bread and gave thanks to God in front of
them all. Then he broke it and began to eat. They were all encouraged and
ate some food themselves. Altogether there were 276 of us on board. When
they had eaten as much as they wanted, they lightened the ship by throw-
ing the grain into the sea.

The men on this ship were in a constant state of fear and suspense for 14
days and had therefore gone without food. They were so afraid and tense that
they just could not eat.

We also see this type of involuntary fasting in 1 Samuel 1:8 (NIV) when
Hannah was so disconsolate over being barren that she couldn't eat. The Bible
says, "Elkanah her husband would say to her, 'Hannah, why are you weeping?
Why don't you eat? Why are you down hearted? Don't I mean more to you
than ten sons?'"

Hannah wanted something else from the Lord. She was so desperate and
distraught that she could not eat. In verse 18, Hannah speaks to Eli, the priest:
"'May your servant find favor in your eyes.' Then she went her way and ate
something, and her face was no longer downcast." Her face was downcast not
because she was fasting but because she was grieving and crying out to God for
a son. When she was assured that her petition was granted, she regained her
appetite.

When you fast you should have a purpose. After your purpose for fasting
has been met, you will feel free to eat. While you may not see the results in the
natural realm, you will sense there has been a breakthrough in the Spirit and
your request has been accomplished.

When Food Is Unavailable

Another involuntary fast is one that happens because no food is available. Once again, we see an example of this in Paul's experiences while spreading the gospel. In 2 Corinthians 11:27 (NIV) he says:

I have labored and toiled and have often gone without sleep; I have known hunger and thirst and have often gone without food...

Another example is one of my favorite female preachers of history, Amanda Smith (1837-1915), a black woman born in slavery. She was a traveling evangelist and had the opportunity to speak where previously no black person had been allowed to speak. She was called "God's image carved in ebony."

She once said, "A good deal of praying fills you up pretty well when you cannot get anything else." There were many times when food was not available to her, and so she was forced to fast involuntarily. She learned to deal with her situation by praying and being filled with God and being sustained in Him.

The Voluntary Fast

The third kind of fast is a voluntary fast. This fast is for the purpose of afflicting your own soul or denying yourself. It was part of the Jewish custom to fast on the Day of Atonement; it was a national day set aside for people to be with God alone.

An example of a voluntary fast is when you petition God for certain things and purpose that you will not eat. He gives you a certain period of time to fast, and He gives you certain things to do, particular directions as you fast.

Sometimes when God leads us on a fast, we completely lose our appetite. We can go through the day and have a wonderful time. And by the end of the day, when it's time for dinner, something happens and we lose our appetite. We had planned on eating, maybe we had even cooked a good meal, but somehow it no longer looks appealing to us. God has ministered to us in a very sovereign way and has taken away our desire for natural food.

Second Samuel 12:22-23 (NIV) says concerning David:

He answered, "While the child was still alive, I fasted and wept. I thought, 'Who knows? The Lord may be gracious to me and let the child live.' But now that he is dead, why should I fast? Can I bring him back again? I will go to him, but he will not return to me."

David had purposed in his heart, "I'm going to fast. I'm going to pray and see if God will have mercy on me regarding the baby I had with Bathsheba." We know the answer. The Lord, in that particular circumstance, said no.

Sometimes fear and distress stir God's people to fast. For instance, during war the Israelites fasted because of fear, stress, and concern. In Judges 20:26, the people responded to war by fasting. In times of war God's people were called upon to fast. Should we do any less?

Another reason for a voluntary fast is to humble yourself, to lower yourself. While we know that only the blood of Jesus Christ (through repentance) can cleanse us from our sins, fasting can be an outward expression of repentance when we engage in this discipline to break a bondage in our lives. It also builds our faith.

Biblical Ways of Fasting

Fasting is a personal, individual interchange between you and the Lord. Don't allow fasting to become a legalistic yoke. If the Holy Spirit leads you, fasting will be very liberating. Let's look at some of the different ways in which God's people fasted in biblical times.

In Judges 20:26 (NIV) we read:

Then the Israelites, all the people, went up to Bethel, and there they sat weeping before the Lord. They fasted that day until evening and presented burnt offerings and fellowship offerings to the Lord.

In Exodus 34:28 (NIV) we read:

Moses was there with the Lord forty days and forty nights without eating bread or drinking water. And he wrote on the tablets the words of the covenant—the Ten Commandments.

Can you imagine going without bread or water for 40 days and 40 nights? And he did it twice! Over these last ten years, there has been a fasting movement in which many people have completed 40-day fasts; yet, none I know of has fasted in the way Moses did.

I have a feeling that Moses was so full, so saturated, so totally one with God, that he could be there on that mount for 40 days and 40 nights and not desire anything but God. I believe that he was literally absorbed in God, caught up into the heavens. I picture a glory cloud there, so covering him that no one could see him but God.

As Elijah fled from Jezebel and traveled to Horeb, he fasted. One of the ways you remove the Jezebel spirit of manipulation and control is to fast!

The angel of the Lord came back a second time and touched him and said, "Get up and eat, for the journey is too much for you." So he got up and ate and drank. Strengthened by that food, he traveled forty days and forty nights until he reached Horeb, the mountain of God. There he went into a cave and spent the night.

—1 Kings 19:7-9, NIV

In the cave, Elijah had a conversation with God. When you fast, you're going to hear God. Elijah got rid of Jezebel, and he went on to hear the still, small voice of God.

In Luke 4:1-4 (NIV), we read:

Jesus, full of the Holy Spirit, returned from the Jordan and was led by the Spirit in the desert, where for forty days he was tempted by the devil. He ate nothing during those days, and at the end of them he was hungry. The devil said to him, "If you are the Son of God, tell this stone to become bread." Jesus answered, "It is written. Man does not live on bread alone."

Jesus had such power and such anointing upon Himself that He could discern when the enemy was using the Word of God to try and trick Him.

How Long Can a Person Fast?

How long can one fast without starving? Well, do not consider Moses on Mount Sinai as an example. He was supernaturally sustained by the Lord, because the human body cannot naturally endure the lack of water for that long a period of time. You'll recall that Moses went for 40 days without water. If you or I attempted to do the same, we would die in a matter of days. Three days is the limit for going without water. Moses was in an extremely unusual heavenly state when he fasted for 40 days.

It is humanly possible to fast with only water for up to 90 days under extreme and supervised conditions. However, under normal conditions, once you have reached 40 days you are starving. David must have been on an extended fast when he said in Psalm 109:24 (NIV): "My knees give way from fasting; my body is thin and gaunt."

There are times you will get physically uncomfortable and weak when you are on a fast, but if you are in a desperate situation the Lord may lead you to continue until there is a breakthrough. In any case, you must be led by God's Holy Spirit.

Take a look at Moses' second fast in Deuteronomy 9:18-21 (NIV):

Then once again I fell prostrate before the Lord for forty days and forty nights; I ate no bread and drank no water, because of all the sin you had committed, doing what was evil in the Lord's sight and so provoking Him to anger. I feared the anger and wrath of the Lord, for He was angry enough with you to destroy you. But again the Lord listened to me. And the Lord was angry enough with Aaron to destroy him but at that time I prayed for Aaron too. Also I took that sinful thing of yours, the calf you had made, and burned it in the fire. Then I crushed it and ground it to powder as fine as dust and threw the dust into a stream that flowed down the mountain.

You see, Moses was fasting because of the sin that was in the camp. He realized that God was so angry that He wanted to kill the people—including Aaron the high priest. This crisis situation was Moses' reason for fasting for 40 days and 40 nights.

In 2 Samuel 3:35 we see David also taking a very serious approach to fasting:

Then they all came and urged David to eat something while it was still day; but David took an oath, saying, "May God deal with me, be it ever so severely, if I taste bread or anything else before the sun sets!"

David took fasting so seriously that he could say, "May God deal with me if I break this fast before my committed time." Here it shows that the Hebrews fasted from sunup to sundown, their customary way of fasting.

If God has called you to go on a fast, it is important that you regard it as a serious matter before the Lord. But be careful not to go on any extended fast unless you are clearly led by the Lord. I also advise checking with your doctor, especially before going on a first-time extended fast. Even though we have examples of fasting for 40 days, most people will not be called to go on such an extended fast, though there are creative ways to do so. Be led by the Holy Spirit in whatever you do.

What Is a Daniel Fast?

During our prayer pilgrimage, we stayed on a type of Daniel fast. This involved eating food, but only in a limited way. Let us look at Daniel 10:2-3 (NIV):

At that time, I Daniel, mourned for three weeks [mourning sometimes represents fasting]. I ate no choice food; no meat or wine touched my lips; and I used no lotions at all until the three weeks were over.

Daniel sought the Lord for 21 days for wisdom, direction, and understanding. He was trying to understand the future. God wanted Daniel to know about things that were going to happen. During this time, Daniel was visited by an angel who gave him insight to understand the vision he had received.

During Daniel's fast, he ate no pleasant food, no delicacies, meat or wine. When you go on this kind of fast, you can still perform your daily tasks. This type of fast is especially ideal if you have a strenuous job or high-stress schedule. On a Daniel fast, you are giving yourself some sustenance without totally weakening yourself.

After being on a Daniel-type fast over a period of time, (up to 21 days if God leads you), you may consider making it a dietary lifestyle from that point on.

Fasting and Your Attitudes

Always examine your motives when you fast. Why not purpose to fast not only from food, but also from the sins that do so easily beset us—those carnal attitudes of judging and finger pointing? (See Isaiah 58.) You may want to consider fasting from talking. You can read more about this type of fast in my book, *Intimacy with the Beloved.*

While fasting, start thinking about the things that come out of your mouth and the things that you do. On occasion I have had to confess to the Lord that I have been a hypocrite in a particular area. Matthew 6:16-18 tells us not to be hypocrites when we fast. Repent and fast from the negative things God reveals to you. Turn your heart totally and sincerely to the Lord. You are in for a refreshing time with God.

The Lord promised that He will not refuse the sacrifice of a broken, contrite heart. Fasting is an effective way to bring brokenness.

Perhaps God has already revealed some things in your life and you have confessed sin. But when you start to fast and pray, He reveals even the "little foxes" that you would not normally see when your flesh is strong. When you fast the power of your flesh gets weaker, and God is enabled to reveal things to you that require keen spiritual discernment. Fasting provides spiritual clarity and focus.

Fasting With Others

Then Esther sent this reply to Mordecai: "Go, gather together all the Jews who are in Susa, and fast for me. Do not eat or drink for three days, night or day. I and my maids will fast as you do. When this is done, I will go to the king, even though it is against the law. And if I perish, I perish."

—Esther 4:15-16, NIV

Esther said, "Fast for me." She was the one interceding for her people. Yet she was not asking them to fast for the people; she was asking them to fast for her. I believe the Lord shows here that it is appropriate to ask someone to fast for you. In this instance, it is acceptable to let others know that you are fasting.

If people are praying or ministering with you and are a part of what you are doing, it is appropriate for them to know that you are fasting. Invite them to join with you as well.

When I travel somewhere on an assignment from the Lord—perhaps to a group of people who need a particular type of ministry from God—I often ask others to fast in support of the assignment. Now note this request is not to fast for the people, but for me, and to pray that God's power, strength, wisdom, or whatever else I need, will equip me so that I can be a tool in God's hand to accomplish His purposes.

Fasting is Good for You

Fasting is a natural, wholesome, healthy lifestyle. As you begin to engage in the discipline of fasting, you will discover some pleasant side effects. Fasting gives your body rest. Have you considered that the word *breakfast* means "to break one's fast?" By not eating overnight while we sleep, we are actually fasting. Breakfast means to take the first food after the night fast. The Lord has planned for natural times of fasting so our digestive systems can rest. He gives us a natural fast, whether we like it or not. When we are sleeping we cannot be eating!

Fasting can even bring healing to your body. When you fast you will find that you are more mentally acute than normal. Those who use a lot of caffeine or sugar may not hear or think better for the first few days because of experiencing withdrawal symptoms. But on the whole, you hear better and think better, spiritually and physically.

Fasting and prayer gives blessed refreshing to your soul. You will identify with the prophet in Jeremiah 15:16 (NKJV): "Your words were found, and I ate them, and Your word was to me a joy and the rejoicing of my heart; for I am called by Your name, O Lord God of hosts."

Fasting to Seek Direction

The early Christians found fasting to be beneficial as far as seeking the will of God and His direction. Acts 13:2-3 (NIV):

While they were worshiping the Lord and fasting, the Holy Spirit said, "Set apart for me Barnabas and Saul for the work to which I have called them." So after they had fasted and prayed, they placed their hands on them and sent them off.

The prophetic word is often much stronger and much clearer when there has been fasting. When we are fasting, there is a greater anointing when we lay hands on a person being set apart for ministry. Acts 14:23 (NIV) says:

Paul and Barnabas appointed elders for them in each church and, with prayer and fasting, committed them to the Lord, in whom they had put their trust.

Your intercession can be more effective when you fast. If you are fasting and praying for a specific situation, that intercession can be very, very powerful. You will be amazed at how clearly you will hear the voice of the Lord.

Here's a word of caution: Test any spiritual voice you hear to be sure that it lines up with Scripture. Check your own motives before God, too. Share what you believe God is saying with mature, stable, and seasoned men and women of God. You don't always have to isolate yourself when you fast. It is good to fast with others as well as alone.

Fasting to Break Bondages

Matthew 17:14-21 talks about a young man who was a demoniac, who experienced epileptic seizures. Jesus explained that this particular bondage did not break except by prayer and fasting.

While you are fasting, not only are you praying for others and lifting them up and asking God to break their bondages, but you are also getting your own life right before God as the sins in your life are exposed to your own heart.

As I travel and speak, whatever kind of fast the Lord prescribes for me I do, because I never know what I will encounter as I minister. I'm open to ministering deliverance if it is needed in order to cast out demons as Jesus did. So I prepare myself in fasting, prayer, worship, and communion with the Lord.

Fasting for Souls

Fasting is very important and very necessary, and can influence souls for eternity. There is hardly any reason why someone cannot fast, unless your doctor has told you not to fast. We need to become concerned not only for our own souls but also for the souls of our Christian brothers and sisters and the world. Nehemiah knew that burden. Note Nehemiah 1:2-4 (NIV):

> *Hanani, one of my brothers, came from Judah with some other men, and I questioned them about the Jewish remnant that survived the exile, and also about Jerusalem. They said to me, "Those who survived the exile and are back in the province are in great trouble and disgrace. The wall of Jerusalem is broken down, and its gates have been burned with fire." When I heard these things, I sat down and wept. For some days I mourned and fasted and prayed before the God of heaven.*

Nehemiah is a wonderful example to us. He wanted to rebuild the walls of Jerusalem. I believe God is calling all of us to do the same: to build the walls of God's Church. We should be so afflicted and troubled in our hearts when we see sin and corruption in the Church that we sit down to weep and cry because the walls have been torn down.

When souls are at stake, the sense of mourning and grieving and crying out to God, the brokenness in our lives, should be such that we are willing to go without food.

God is not impressed with our fasting in itself. He is not impressed with our physical posture of getting on our faces or getting on our knees. These things can become just religious exercises if they are not done by the anointing of the Holy Spirit. But when we come before God in brokenness and humility in the anointing of the Spirit, our actions become awesome, holy, and very powerful!

Fasting is for the purpose of breaking every yoke of bondage. But when you fast, you rend your heart instead of your garment. We need to allow our hearts to be torn by the Lord.

How to Prepare for a Fast

There are certain things you can do in the natural to ensure your success in fasting. Remember that each of us is at a different stage of development in God. Therefore, never let yourself come under condemnation about fasting. Some of us can stop eating at a moment's notice, fast, and have no problems. For others it is more difficult.

Here are some very practical suggestions before you begin your fast.

1. Before you decide to go on a fast, I would highly recommend that you see your doctor. You need to know the condition of your health.

2. Ask God for His anointing and His empowering before you fast. You cannot do this alone, but with God's help you can succeed. Also, ask God for His cleansing while you are going through a fast. If you need healing—physical, spiritual, or emotional—He can meet these needs as you draw closer to Him in prayer.

3. Define the purpose of your fast. There should be a reason for your fast. Ask yourself: what is my heart's motivation? Why are you doing it?

4. Pray and ask God for His chosen fast. What kind of fast does He want you to go on and how long will it last? He may say just one meal today. He may say three days, or He may say ten days. Ask Him when to start your fast. Sometimes He desires to prepare your heart and body before you start a fast.

5. When you prepare your body for a fast, one of the first things to do is to gradually reduce your intake of sugar and caffeine. Replace

the sugar with fruit. In order to avoid headaches, mental confusion, and sluggishness, gradually start eliminating caffeine. Your body must be weaned gradually from these foods until it is ready to go without them. That means reduce your daily two to three cups of coffee to one cup. The next day reduce that to one-half cup, then one-fourth, until you are off caffeine.

6. I highly recommend that you drink lots of water to prepare for fasting and throughout your fast. Your body builds up toxins during those first few days and will need to clean itself out. Drinking lots of water will help to flush out those toxins from your body.

Ending Your Fast

After fasting for several days you may discover that you are enjoying a release of His anointing and a sense of His presence. Be alert and let the Lord lead you when to end the fast. Be encouraged that the benefits after fasting, although perhaps not as pronounced as during a fast, will endure for a long time.

If you go on an extended fast, you need to know how to come off the fast. I've had some marvelous times of fasting, yet have ended the fast improperly. This has happened when I've eaten the wrong things when coming off a fast.

When ending a fast, stay away from spicy foods. If you are on a water-only fast, break it by starting to drink juice. Some people break a fast by eating yogurt. It's nice to have fresh fruit or fresh vegetables if possible. Steamed vegetables are good, too. Plain food without a lot of seasoning is also good. One of the most energizing foods after a fast is fresh carrot juice, which has a stabilizing effect on the body.

The most important advice I can give you is this: Whatever you do, do not overeat! Many people miss some of the physical benefits of an extended fast because afterwards they immediately begin to overeat. Be careful that this does not happen to you.

If you have lost weight while you were fasting, begin now to eat properly and your body will maintain an ideal weight for you. It's as if God gives us the opportunity to cleanse our systems and get back to the physical size and dietary lifestyle that He intended. As you see, even though we fast primarily for spiritual purposes, fasting also has its physical benefits.

Our God is a very practical God. He is God of the whole person. Yield your whole life to Him and let Him direct your path. Remember, He is the one who is able to keep you blameless in spirit, soul, and body.

Drawing Closer to God Through Fasting

As you journey to the secret places of God's own heart, you will quickly discover that fasting is a powerful tool for entering into new and greater dimensions of God. Fasting is more than not eating; it is a total response to the promptings of the Holy Spirit. You are responding as David did when he said, "When Thou didst say, 'Seek My face,' my heart said to Thee, 'Thy face, O Lord, I shall seek'" (Ps. 27:8).

Fasting is for the purpose of possessing Jesus our Lord, fulfilling His will and purposes as a holy remnant, a Bride awaiting the Bridegroom. Fasting will help to bring a great outpouring of Holy Spirit glory.

If you are one who is already seeking the Lord in fasting, I pray that you will continue to be encouraged in this discipline. If you have not experienced fasting in the past, I pray that you will be motivated to begin a new lifestyle of seeking the Lord in prayer, worship, reading His Word, and fasting.

Oswald Chambers said, "You are getting tired of life as it is, tired of yourself as you are, getting sour with regard to the setting of your life; lift your eyes for one moment to Jesus Christ. Do you want, more than you want your food, more than you want your sleep, more than you want anything under heaven, or in heaven, that Jesus Christ might so identify you with Himself that you are His first and last and for ever? God grant that the great longing desire of your heart may begin to awaken as it has never done, not only the desire for the forgiveness of sin, but the identification with Jesus Himself until you say, 'I live, yet not I, but Christ liveth in me'" (Gal. 2:20).[1]

✎ ENDNOTE ✎

1. Oswald Chambers; *Still Higher for His Highest*; Zondervan; Grand Rapids, Michigan; 1971; p.68.

Chapter Five

UNDISTRACTED DEVOTION

And this I say for your own benefit; not to put a restraint upon you, but to promote what is seemly, and to secure undistracted devotion to the Lord.

—1 Corinthians 7:35

single white phone hung on the wall facing the open kitchen. Above it was a carefully placed note providing directions for making an emergency phone call, which was still possible from this special connection arrangement despite the fact that the phone service had not been turned on. There could be no telephone calls—except that one call when we arrived to let our families know that we were safe. More importantly, the television would never be turned on, there would be no purchasing of newspapers or magazines, and cell phones would be disabled. Furthermore, we would not be hooked up to the Internet. Most interestingly, we sensed that the Lord was even limiting our conversations. The spiritual climate of this week shut in with God would be carefully guarded from the world and the flesh.

As you seek to press into a new level in God, you will quickly discover that distractions are one of the devil's first and greatest weapons to hinder you. Therefore, you must be prepared to guard against them and do all you can to minimize the distractions before they occur.

The Enemy's Weapon

In the book of Nehemiah, while the people of God were working to rebuild the walls of Jerusalem after they had been destroyed, their enemies plotted to keep the work from progressing. One of the key weapons they used was to create distractions in order to hinder the progress of the builders. "Now it came about when Sanballat, Tobiah, and the Arabs, the Ammonites, and the Ashdodites heard that the repair of the walls of Jerusalem went on, and that the breaches began to be closed, they were very angry. And all of them conspired together to come and fight against Jerusalem and to cause a disturbance in it," (Neh. 4:7-8).

The enemies of God and the enemies of His people planned to create enough of a disturbance to distract those who were building so that the job could not be completed.

The enemy's devices are never new, but we are "wary of his devices" (2 Cor. 2:11), including his craftiness and deceitful schemes (see Eph. 6:11). That's why we must realize that "our struggle is not against flesh and blood, but against the rulers, the powers, against the world forces of this darkness, against the spiritual forces of wickedness in heavenly places" (Eph. 6:12). You can be sure that your enemy, the devil, does not want you to enter into a new level in God. For when you touch God, you bring His purposes and plans into the earth, and your victory in prayer marks the devil's defeat.

So, be aware that he may try to fight you, and one of the major ways of doing that is through distractions. Therefore, to insure success be prepared to guard against them.

Distractions will break down the hedge of protection that God has built up around your prayer time, and this generally occurs through the carnal and mundane. Those things we would consider perfectly harmless at other times can become hindrances to prayer for no other reason than they take our focus off the Lord and place it on self, the world, or on the flesh.

This doesn't mean that newspapers are wicked or television is of the devil. Such things are not always bad, but when you are pressing into the Spirit of God, they can create a worldly draw upon your spirit man that can hold you back by distracting your focus and dissipating your spiritual strength. Entering into the depths of God requires your total focus, so you must guard yourself from distractions.

Just a Little Leaven

Proverbs 25:26 says, "Like a trampled spring and a polluted well is a righteous man who gives way before the wicked." Do you realize that only a little poison can destroy the water supply of an entire city? Allowing just a little pollution into your sanctified, hallowed time with the Lord can pollute the entire wonderful time of refreshing and intimacy you have planned with God. Remember, just a little leaven leavens the whole lump (see 1 Cor. 5:6). On the other hand, the spiritual atmosphere of Heaven can also be like leaven. We have the opportunity to spread the atmosphere of Heaven (our leaven) after we've experienced refreshing times with our Lord.

There is a deposit from Heaven that the enemy knows God has placed within us. This deposit is activated like leaven; the deposit matures and changes us completely. We ourselves then become a deposit from Heaven into the earth to affect everyone around us. We are leaven that should change the world around us. We are lights to brighten the way of others. By maintaining the proper spiritual focus in life, we can also "leaven the whole lump," or dramatically impact the world.

Guard Precious Times With God

Second Timothy 2:4 is a wonderful passage of Scripture that applies directly to this matter: "No soldier in active service entangles himself in the affairs of everyday life, so that he may please the one who enlisted him as a soldier." According to the apostle Paul, there are times when it is not appropriate to be overly concerned with the details of daily life. Worldly concerns can consume our focus and distract our attention away from God. Consequently, we must draw away for a season, so that we will be free from the distractions of daily life in order to totally focus on the lover of our souls.

Then, when we return to our normal, everyday life, we will be better equipped to do the things necessary to handle these distractions. We will have a different point of view. What was once overwhelming will become more manageable because we will consider it with an entirely new perspective.

The Bible says, "How blessed is the one whom Thou dost choose, and bring near to Thee, to dwell in Thy courts. We will be satisfied with the goodness of Thy house, Thy holy temple" (Ps. 65:4).

Your deep desire to enter into a deeper place of intimacy with the Lord is like a calling card. It is an indication that He has invited you to join Him in the depths of holiness, the secret places of His glorious presence.

Coming into the secret places of God is a holy trust, one that must be carefully guarded. Second Timothy 1:14 says, "Guard, through the Holy Spirit who dwells in us, the treasure which has been entrusted to you." The Lord spoke to me years ago and said, "Guard the anointing. Be careful how you handle what I have entrusted to you." We must hold precious our relationship with our Lord and treasure our intimate walk.

Intimacy with our beloved Lord Jesus must always be highly prized, guarded carefully from the draws of sin and the world. We must carefully protect and develop what He has placed within us to the measure of our calling and usefulness in the Kingdom of God and the world. Jesus is the treasure, our relationship is the treasure, His gifts and calling are the treasure; and it all belongs to Him.

By purposefully minimizing distractions, even being careful of what you talk about, you will be guarding the greatest treasure that exists—Heaven's treasure.

Guard Your Attitude

Your success at entering into the depths of Jesus Christ will largely be determined by your attitude. Hence, it's very important to come before God in the right frame of mind. If you choose a time to seek the Lord, but haven't been away from the family for years, and decide it is also a great time to have a weeklong pajama party or nonstop shopping trip, you may leave disappointed in your desire to go deeper into God.

Paul warned Timothy to guard the treasure that had been entrusted to him. *Guard* in the Greek language means "to prevent from escaping, to watch or preserve." It means "to keep safe, to guard from injury or loss by keeping one's eye upon, to hold fast or to keep."

Paul would not have warned Timothy to guard the treasure of God's Spirit if loss were not a possibility. So, enter into this time with a sober, focused, and guarded attitude, determined that nothing will distract you from your objective, which is to draw closer to God. "Be dressed in readiness, and keep your lamps alight. And be like men who are waiting for the master when he returns from the wedding feast, so that they may immediately open the door to him when he comes and knocks. Blessed are those slaves whom the master shall find on the alert when he comes" (Luke 12:35-37). And Luke 17:3 adds: "Be on your guard! If your brother sins, rebuke him; and if he repents, forgive him."

The Bible strongly urges us to be very cautious in how we walk, and to use our time very wisely, not frittering it away with empty pursuits, especially when we have set our purpose to come before the throne of God. Ephesians 5:15-16 warns: "Be careful how you walk, not as unwise men but as wise, making the most of your time because the days are evil."

The Bible carefully warns us that we must remain alert and vigilant in order to pray successfully, not allowing ourselves to become weighed down with dissipation, drunkenness and worries. First Peter 4:7 says, "...be of sound judgment and sober spirit for the purpose of prayer." *Sound judgment* means "self-control, self-restraint, using wisdom, prudence, and discernment."

The End of All Things is at Hand

The *end of all things* means the "culmination of all things." The Lord is calling all of us to be open and willing to do great things for Him, to go to the next step in devotion and service. Are you willing?

Because we are coming toward the end of all events in the history of mankind, we must pray in order to receive greater power and more authority. We must be able to move quickly at the Lord's Word, and we must be spiritually strong enough to overcome the enemy's weapons sent to distract and hinder us. By doing these things, we will gain a greater inner walk with God that will significantly change our outer walk, too.

Since the 9/11 disaster at the World Trade Center in New York and the Pentagon in Washington, D.C., many people are saying that our nation will never again be the same. The world has changed; now more than ever, the Lord has need of us. This new season in the world will require from us a higher and deeper relationship with Jesus Christ. We will need to bear greater fruit of discernment, power, authority, wisdom, and understanding. It is vital in these times that we are people of great prayer. Indeed, we are the light of the world. We are the only light that the world has, and the times are getting darker than we realize.

According to the Word of God, a city set on a hill should not be hidden. Now more than ever before, we must not allow the light of glory within us to be hidden under distractions, worldly concerns, and frivolous pursuits. We are the salt of the earth, according to Matthew 5:13-14. The salt of our relationship with Jesus must make the world thirsty for Him in this hour of great need.

We are warned not to let down our guard because of the difficult times in which we are living: "Be on guard, that your hearts may not be weighed down with dissipation and drunkenness and the worries of life, and that day come on you suddenly like a trap; for it will come upon all those who dwell on the face of all the earth. But keep on the alert at all times, praying in order that you may have strength to escape all these things that are about to take place, and to stand before the Son of Man" (Luke 21:34-36).

Dissipation, drunkenness, and worries are three traps that the Lord warns against. These are the distractions that could cause you to lose God's best for you during this time of prayer by diverting your purpose and objective.

Worries

Worries speak of the cares of this life and the deceitfulness of sin. When you leave for your prayer pilgrimage, simply be sure to put everything in order. Leave your children and spouse with an emergency plan in case anything goes wrong. And, before you leave, put them in God's hands and know in your heart that He is well able to care for them in your absence.

Don't leave coworkers with an expectation that you will do work while you are away, and communicate to your family the importance of minimizing phone calls. Set up a prearranged time for you to make calls to your family.

Now, set your mind to not worry about anything you've left behind. This is your special time alone with God, so don't let the devil create a distraction for you that robs you of your blessing through worry.

Dissipation

Dissipation means "to cause to spread out or spread thin to the point of vanishing; to lose (as heat or electricity) irrecoverably; to expend aimlessly or foolishly; to separate into parts and scatter or vanish; to be extravagant in the pursuit of pleasure; and to scatter or waste."

It's not difficult to see how we dissipate the spiritual empowerment and assignments that God gives us. In 2 Kings 4:29, the prophet Elisha told his servant Gehazi to "Salute no man" when Gehazi was filled with healing power in order to lay Elisha's staff on the face of a dead child. Jesus actually said the same thing to His disciples when He sent them out to minister. In other words, don't be drawn away or distracted from your purpose.

Oswald Chambers said, "The fundamental basis of the human will deep down is inclined towards God, and prayer works wonders fundamentally. The prayer of the feeblest saint on earth who lives in the Spirit and keeps right with God is a terror to satan. The very powers of darkness are paralyzed by prayer, no spiritualistic séance can succeed in the presence of a humble praying saint. No wonder satan tries to keep our minds fussy in active work till we cannot think in prayer. It is a vital necessity for Christians to think along the lines on which they pray. The philosophy of prayer is that prayer is the work."[1]

It's important to understand when you have a spiritual assignment from God that involves moving deeply into spiritual things, you must stay focused. Don't stop to visit with numerous friends along the way or shop for several hours—until you sense a release to do so. There will come a time during your prayer journey that you will sense a release to get out and walk or shop or go have lunch. But be very sure that you have reached your spiritual objectives before you do.

Dissipation involves wasting or throwing away the anointing or spiritual energy and focus that God has given you by trying to do too many things that God has not assigned you to do. Remember that reaching your spiritual goals and objectives in the long run will be far more rewarding than spending precious hours shopping, visiting, or reading worldly publications.

Drunkenness

Consider for a minute what it means to be drunk in the natural. You are partaking of a spirit that dulls your ability to react, dulls your senses and ability to think, and dulls your ability to see and your ability to have proper control.

Prayer at the level that we're speaking of requires a real degree of sobriety. First Peter 4:7 says, "…be of sound judgment and sober." Entering into the glorious presence of a holy God should not be done lightly. This same theme is found again in 1 Thessalonians 5:6: "So then let us not sleep as others do, but let us be alert and sober." And again, 1 Peter 5:8 says, "Be of sober spirit, be on the alert. Your adversary, the devil, prowls about like a roaring lion, seeking someone to devour."

Each of these passages underscores the seriousness and guarded manner in which we should embark upon a time of prayer. Such moments of intimacy with a holy God is not something that should ever be taken lightly. Arm yourself with an attitude of seriousness, holiness, and focus. We must be diligent to guard our souls: "Only give heed to yourself and keep your soul diligently, lest you forget the things which your eyes have seen, and lest they depart from your heart all the days of your life" (Deut. 4:9).

Guard Your Tongue

One of the most important ways of preparing yourself for this holy journey is by guarding your speech. This is found in one of my favorite passages of Scripture:

> *Guard your steps as you go to the house of God, and draw near to listen rather than to offer the sacrifice of fools; for they do not know they are doing evil. Do not be hasty in word or impulsive in thought to bring up a matter in the presence of God. For God is in heaven and you are on the earth; therefore let your words be few.*
>
> —Ecclesiastes 5:1-2

What you say or don't say will prove a powerful key for entering into the depths of Jesus Christ. This passage suggests that speaking impulsively or foolishly is actually seen before the throne of glory as evil.

Remember when Jesus took Peter, James, and John to the Mount of Transfiguration where they saw Christ transfigured and speaking with Elijah and Moses? Poor Peter, who had so much trouble getting control over his spirit and tongue, blurted out, "Oh, Lord. It's good that we're here 'cause we'll make three monuments." God Almighty spoke a rebuke from Heaven to Peter, which I'm sure was very sobering. (See Matt. 17:1-6.)

Guarding our tongues during this holy pilgrimage into God's presence is an essential key for determining your success. Paul carefully warned Timothy about this matter. He said, "Oh, Timothy, guard what has been entrusted to you, avoiding worldly and empty chatter" (1 Tim. 6:20). Again, he says, "But avoid worldly and empty chatter, for it will lead to further ungodliness" (2 Tim. 2:16).

Don't spend your time gossiping and talking about worldly matters. Don't select a prayer partner who lacks control in these areas, for you can absolutely lose the blessing God desires to give you by chatting it away through empty small talk.

David knew how important this matter of talking too much or talking about the wrong things could be. He cried out to God with a prayer that we should all pray before we begin such a holy experience. He said, "May my prayer be counted as incense before Thee; the lifting up of my hands as the evening offering. Set a guard, O Lord, over my mouth; keep watch over the door of my lips" (Ps. 141:2-3).

David realized that for his prayer to be sweet and precious before the Lord, he needed to be extremely careful not to speak carelessly or foolishly in God's presence.

Why is what we say so important? The spirit of the world is transferred through our words. Empty, worldly, and hurtful speech deeply wounds the Holy Spirit. "Let no unwholesome word proceed from your mouth, but only such a word as is good for edification according to the need of the moment, that it may give grace to those who hear. And do not grieve the Holy Spirit of

God, by whom you were sealed for the day of redemption" (Eph. 4:29-30). In this passage we see that what we say or don't say is directly linked to grieving the Holy Spirit. How can we draw close to the Holy Spirit in prayer while at the same time push Him away through worldly chatter? It's impossible. Therefore, we must carefully guard our speech.

Our tongues defile our entire bodies because they are set ablaze from the fires of hell (see James 3:6). That is reason enough to be very careful of what we say while we're entering into this holy time of prayer.

Start your prayer pilgrimage with the same declaration that David made: "I have purposed that my mouth will not transgress" (Ps. 17:3).

A Devoted Time

This time of prayer is a time of total devotion to God. Paul said, "And this I say for your own benefit; not to put a restraint upon you, but to promote what is seemly, and to secure undistracted devotion to the Lord" (1 Cor. 7:35). To be devoted suggests being separated from everything else but that thing to which you're exclusively loyal.

If I'm devoted to my family, then my spouse and children are the focus of my life and emotions. If I'm devoted to my job, my attention and energy will be expended there. Similarly, during this day or week of prayer, your total devotion needs to be God's alone, not shopping, vacationing, visiting, talking, cooking, sightseeing, etc. This is His day or week; therefore, you must set your heart and mind to be completely devoted to Him. Such devotion is the key to success.

Devotion means separation. We find an powerful example of this in Acts 13:2: "Set apart for me Barnabas and Saul for the work to which I have called them." Their lives, time, energy, and resources would be wholly given to the ministry that God called them to.

Separation is a key to spiritual power. When we're called to prayer, we're called to separation. Separation is also a synonym for holiness. To be holy simply means that your life is separated to God. You are devoted to Him and not to the world and its purposes and pleasures. We who are believers are a holy nation and a chosen people (see 1 Peter 2:9). God has separated His people from out of the nations of the earth. We are "called out" from others. Leviticus 20:24 says, "I am the Lord your God, who has separated you from the peoples." God has designated that you and I might be a different kind of people, ones who are completed committed, devoted, and in love with our sweet and wonderful Master.

Just where did He get the right to all of this love and devotion? He paid the price on Calvary through His own death. We are bought with a heavy price as vessels of honor. "You are not your own...you have been bought with a price; therefore glorify God in your body" (1 Cor. 6:19-20).

Declare Your Intention

As you begin this time of deep prayer and intimacy with God, start by doing a little soul-searching. Ask yourself what are your motives and purposes in selecting a day or week of prayer? Are you trying to make an impression on a prayer leader or to attempt to gain favor with another person? Are you going away because you need a break from your family? Are you going for a vacation?

Consecrate your heart and purposes before God in prayer. Ask Him to search your heart and reveal any worldly or empty reasons for entering into this time. Now declare to Jesus, the lover of your soul, your desire to draw near to Him, to seek Him, to love Him, and to know Him better and more deeply than you've ever known Him.

Tell Him that you are seeking to be utterly devoted, consecrated, and holy in His sight. Ask the Holy Spirit to help you to prepare your mind, heart, and attitude for this time with the heavenly Bridegroom. Ask the Lord to help you to discern what details might become hindrances to you during this special time.

After you've done these things, prepare your heart for the most wonderful, exciting, intimate, spiritual encounter with your heavenly Bridegroom that you've ever imagined. Remember, "Eye has not seen and ear has not heard, and which have not entered the heart of man, all that God has prepared for those who love him" (1 Cor. 2:9).

A Jealous Bridegroom

Our Lord expects and deserves undistracted devotion. He is a jealous heavenly Bridegroom who wants the very best of our time and our love.

For I am jealous for you with a godly jealousy; for I betrothed you to one husband, that to Christ I might present you as a pure virgin. But I am afraid, lest as the serpent deceived Eve by his craftiness, your minds should be led astray from the simplicity and purity of devotion to Christ.

—2 Corinthians 11:2-3

This Scripture depicts the very essence of Paul's apostolic calling. Paul constantly exhorts and encourages others in the Christian community to live in the simplicity and purity of deep, heartfelt love and devotion to Christ. From this simple and pure relationship with Him flows all ministry and life.

As you enter the Lord's presence with holiness, sobriety, humility, and love, you will find that He will not disappoint you. Prepare to be touched with the glorious kiss of divine, supernatural love.

✎ ENDNOTE ✎

1. Oswald Chambers; *Still Higher for His Highest*, Zondervan; Grand Rapids, Michigan; 1971; p. 89.

Chapter Six

I Will Give Thee Thanks

Enter His gates with thanksgiving, and His courts with praise. Give thanks to Him; bless His name.

—Psalm 100:4

We have spent the early morning exploring, walking up and down the breathtaking shoreline of the Pacific Ocean. Refreshed and bursting with the sights and sounds of God's glorious creation, we return to our cottage where we lay down our handfuls of picked flowers next to sofa chairs in the sitting area of my bedroom. I'm sensing that familiar wooing of the Holy Spirit calling me into prayer, and nothing else matters but responding to Him.

The fresh mountain air is still, and we've already spent most of the week praying, worshiping, reading the Word of God and pressing into His wonderful presence. Each time we've prayed, the anointing of His presence has increased—gotten a little thicker, more tangible. It's as if we've been journeying beyond our usual reality and advancing, by stages, into the world of the Spirit.

The pressing into His presence has also gotten increasingly easy. A cloud of glory descends upon us, blanketing us like a thick blanket of peace. Now, His presence is glorious, and the revelation of the Holy Spirit is mighty. We feel so full, so blessed, so supernaturally privileged to have entered into this secret place of God. We are overawed by gratitude.

Effortlessly, naturally, as an outflow of the gratitude we feel, we enter into a place of worship that is beyond what we normally experience.

Worshiping Jesus in the Beauty of Holiness

At some point as you press into the depths of God, I believe that there will be a giving over of yourself—of everything that's within you. There is a place where you can worship absolutely, completely from the depths of your heart, soul, spirit, and flesh. I call it just being lost in God. It's when every cell within you is being exerted toward God. It takes all your physical might and mental might—everything. This was one of those times.

Holy, Holy, Holy

Although our physical bodies are always on earth, our spirits actually truly enter the divine realm of God where they join with real angels in their worship of our wonderful Lord before the throne. Sometimes I believe we've heard the throne room mentioned so lightly in connection with our worship that we take this experience casually. There are times in the Spirit when you become aware that you are truly there, worshiping right before Him, kneeling in the midst of myriads of angels, crying "Holy, holy, holy," together with them.

We enter into angelic heavenly worship (see Isa. 6:3). Just as the angels, the cherubim and seraphim were made for this type of worship. Oh, how much more are we who are redeemed by His grace and created in His image made to worship the Creator of the entire universe? This is the same type of worship recorded in the Book of Revelation where a great multitude worshiped Him saying, "Hallelujah! Salvation and glory and power belong to our God" (Rev. 19:1).

It was also the worship of the 24 elders:

The twenty-four elders will fall down before Him who sits on the throne and will worship Him who lives forever and ever, and will cast their crowns before the throne, saying, "Worthy art Thou, our Lord, and our God, to receive glory and honor and power; for Thou didst create all things, and because of Thy will they existed, and were created."

—Revelation 4:10-11

At such times we lose the perception of earth, and all our senses become filled with the spiritual realm. We are truly there with Him, swept up into the heavenlies where all we can do is cry "holy, holy, holy" from the very depths of our being—from the Holy Spirit within us. Our entire bodies and souls shake as we cry out, "Holy, holy, holy." We couldn't speak anything else even if we wanted to. We've entered into the glory realm of Heaven.

The Glory Realm

It was to this very place that Isaiah was swept up as is recorded in Isaiah 6:1-4.

In the year of King Uzziah's death, I saw the Lord sitting on the throne, lofty and exalted, with the train of His robe filling the temple. Seraphim stood above Him, each having six wings; with two he covered his face, and with two he covered his feet, and with two he flew. And one called out to another and said, "Holy, Holy, Holy, is the Lord of hosts, the whole earth is full of His glory." And the foundations of the thresholds trembled at the voice of him who called out, while the temple was filling with smoke.

This place of deepest worship is marked by the outcries of the angels and of your own spirit. Here, Isaiah said that one angel calls out to another, "Holy, holy, holy is the Lord of hosts. The whole earth is full of His glory."

This is a thunderous, angelic place where worship is loud and sustained. Here, your own cries of worship will take every atom of strength within your being—spiritually, emotionally and physically. It is a great, shaking place of holy worship.

But know this, that one enters this place of worship through genuine, Holy Ghost-inspired thankfulness. It is when your heart fills with such gratitude that it overflows and becomes anointed by God that your spirit soars to this thunderous place of worship. Isaiah 6:4 says, "And the foundations of the thresholds trembled at the voice of him who called out, while the temple was filling with smoke." The whole earth fills with God's glory as the angels cry out from this realm.

When you touch this realm, powerful things happen in Heaven and on earth. God's awesome glory is released on earth and the foundations of sin and wickedness are shaken. Principalities and powers topple and fall. In addition, the temple of God fills with smoke. That smoke represents the prayers of God's people. Glory, incense, and power from Heaven are released and come down to earth from this powerful, wonderful place.

It seems so unusual that the gate to this holy place is not found in powerful choirs or armies of prayer warriors. Instead, the key to enter is found in genuine thanksgiving and gratefulness that comes from deep within, which is touched and anointed by the Holy Spirit because of its innocence and purity. We enter the gates of His glory realm with thanksgiving and His courts with praise.

While the angels cry, all of Heaven and earth shake, and the temple fills with Shekinah glory. The glory, the vapor, the cloud, God's incense fills you and fills the place. Adoring prayers and praises bring forth the Shekinah glory. The Shekinah glory is so brilliant, so bright and shiny that the temple is filled with smoke. The smoke and the cloud and the vapor come to literally soften the brilliance of the glory. The whole earth is full of His glory, but the glory itself is so brilliant that Isaiah couldn't help but say, "Woe is me for I am ruined" (see Isa. 6:5). As we see, the glory also brings with it conviction of sin.

The Glory

There is a glory of the world and there is the glory of God. Sometimes, we've not been able to distinguish between the two and mistake the glory of God for the glory of man. Some of us are caught up in our own glory—honor, praise and worship of ourselves. As a result, there is no room for His glory to be seen. In our services and coming together, we may conjure up our own glory, and create a "strange fire" or a counterfeit because we are too impatient to wait for the real thing (see Lev. 10:1). We are too pleased and satisfied with our own creation—an imitation.

The world's form of glory stimulates and motivates us to compete, control, and strive to be higher than others. We desire to receive the accolades and praise from man; whereas, the genuine glory invokes and mandates that we bow low and recognize our own unworthiness and nothingness. Then the Lord receives all attention and focus. We will, in all humility, delight in the Lord receiving all attention and give Him all the praise! May we serve Him only, be willing to do what He wants us to do, and not serve ourselves.

And Jesus answered and said to him, "It is written, 'You shall worship the Lord your God and serve Him only' " (Luke 4:8).

Until we worship and serve Him only, we will not see, handle, nor carry His glory to the level that He so desires for us. We have been doing public ministry, but we have not always been *ready* to do so. May we handle the things of God appropriately by the principles of the Word in our public ministry.

And he led Him to Jerusalem and had Him stand on the pinnacle of the temple, and said to Him, "If You are the Son of God, throw Yourself down from here; for it is written, 'He will give His angels charge concerning you to guard you,' and, 'On their hands they will bear you up, lest you strike your foot against a stone'" (Luke 4:9-11).

One of the greatest detriments to the glory of God in the Body of Christ is to place leaders or any other person on a pedestal. As the enemy deceives us, we set each other on a pinnacle where we worship each other's talents, gifts, and personalities instead of the personhood of our Lord Jesus Christ. However, we are not able to determine the Lord's tolerance level or when He will decide that it's time for someone to fall off their prideful pinnacle. Soon, another may foolishly climb up on that pedestal and likewise say, "It's my turn, let me have my time. What's in this for me?" We don't always learn lessons from the mistakes of others and consequently we continue to challenge the Lord. We attempt to take His place by saying, "Who is the greatest? Can I be?"

And Jesus answered and said to him, "It is said, 'You shall not put the Lord your God to the test.'"...And Jesus returned to Galilee in the power of the Spirit; and news about Him spread through all the surrounding district. And He began teaching in their synagogues and was praised by all.

—Luke 4:12,14-15

Rather than sacrificing His glory, we should sacrifice ourselves. When we pass this spiritual test, news will spread about us. God Himself will exalt us, and other people will praise us because the glory of God rests upon us and not upon anything of ourselves. We will be more fit to do the ministry He has for us. Our hidden ministry to the Lord will be strengthened and our public ministry will come in a higher form. Without compromise, we will declare very clearly who Jesus is. We will be trusted by God to carry and display His glory, proclaiming the year of the Lord. We will not be displaying our own wares, but we will be displaying His glory instead—the reason we exist.

May we humbly say what is written in Luke 4:18-19:

"The Spirit of the Lord is upon Me, because He has anointed Me to preach the gospel to the poor. He has sent Me to proclaim release to the captives, and recovery of sight to the blind, to set free those who are downtrodden, to proclaim the favorable year of the Lord."

This is the way of Jesus, full of authority and power—as He Himself declared: "...Today this Scripture has been fulfilled in your hearing" (Luke 4:21, NAS). My prayer is that this Scripture be fulfilled in us.

Building an Altar of Worship

During this brief season of pressing into God with everything that's within us, we are building an altar of prayer and worship. Have you ever built an altar of prayer in your life? Perhaps you've done so and simply not realized it. Let's look.

Exodus 17:8-15:

Then Amalek came and fought against Israel at Rephidim. So Moses said to Joshua, "Choose men for us, and go out, fight against Amalek. Tomorrow I will station myself on the top of the hill with the staff of God in my hand." And Joshua did as Moses told him, and fought against Amalek; and Moses, Aaron, and Hur went up to the top of the hill. So it came about when Moses held his hand up, that Israel prevailed, and when he let his hand down, Amalek prevailed. But Moses' hands were heavy. Then they took a stone and put it under him, and he sat on it; and Aaron and Hur supported his hands, one on one side and one on the other.

Thus his hands were steady until the sun set. So Joshua overwhelmed Amalek and his people with the edge of the sword. Then the Lord said to Moses, "Write this in a book as a memorial, and recite it to Joshua, that I will utterly blot out the memory of Amalek from under heaven." And Moses built an altar, and named it The Lord is My Banner.

In verse 15 it's interesting to learn that Moses built an altar and named it "The Lord is My Banner." When we take this kind of prayer journey with God, we also build a spiritual altar, and the Lord may give a name to it according to the type of ministry or work He is trying to establish or build in our lives and spirit.

Just as Moses declared that the Lord was his banner, so does the Song of Solomon tell us that His banner over us is love (see Song 2:4). "The Lord is My Banner," means that He is with us in a very, very special way. He is constantly near to us, hovering over us, covering us with His wonderful, delightful presence. The passage in the Song of Solomon lets us know that the Lord is covering us, hovering over us with gentle love and kindness, mercy and constant interest. His thoughts are toward us continually. His favor flows in our direction.

The Lord will also make us His army with banners (see Song 6:4,10). Once we receive the Lord as banner, then we become a banner of love and lovely to look at. We become one who grows like the dawn, beautiful as the moon and pure as the sun. We become like Him in His characteristics. By beholding Him in the depths of worship, we reflect the lovely One whom we behold.

As intercessors, we often look at this Exodus passage in terms of our position next to a leader. Moses was the leader whom Aaron and Hur stood next to, holding up his arms when he tired. As intercessors, we're often called to stand in a position of prayer next to a leader or ministry, in addition to so much more.

Moses, Aaron, and Hur built an altar of God's presence to help Joshua win the battle against Amalek, the enemy of God's people. While Joshua was down in the trenches fighting, three people were involved in a mighty act of intercession.

This story represents how spiritual power works. We pray before God and touch His presence mightily through prayer, in intercessory worship or harp and bowl worship (see Rev. 5:8-9). This worshipful praying brings a new song interwoven with prayer and worship and worship and prayer. You become unable to tell where one leaves off and the other begins. That act releases the victory into the earth over the enemies of God's people. Those who are down in the trenches fighting feel the effect, and satan and his demonic hordes are sent running. Their strongholds are pulled down and their assignments are cancelled.

Later God told Moses to write a book telling how He blotted out the name of Amalek from under Heaven. I believe that this book also is a memorial to the Lord, that He blesses us as we've taken time to come up here to pray, wait, and spend quality time listening to Him, worshipping Him, waiting upon Him, and basking in His wonderful presence.

As others read this book, they may get away to pray and write about their prayer times in their own journals. I believe that God is saying that much has been accomplished in the heavenly realm, that a lot of battles have been won while we've taken the time to come away and be with the Lord.

While we're praying up here on this mountain, there are battles raging in the valleys, and the Joshuas down there may never realize it, but they will feel the effects of this great prayer and intercessory worship.

This mighty place where Heaven touches earth during our times of worshipful prayer has a much greater result than simply making us feel good and closer to God. This great intercession and worship releases angelic hosts into the earth to do battle against the enemies of God.

Do you recall the altar that Jacob built to the Lord at Bethel, otherwise known as Jacob's ladder? Jacob fell asleep with his head on a stone and dreamed that angels of the Lord were ascending and descending above where he slept. He awoke and said, "Surely the Lord is in this place, and I did not know it." How awesome is this place! This is none other than the house of God, and this is the gate of heaven" (Gen. 28:16-17). Later, in Genesis 35:1, we see that the place where Jacob had his dream became an altar. "Then God said to Jacob, 'Arise, go up to Bethel, and live there; and make an altar there to God, who appeared to you when you fled from your brother Esau.'"

Jacob experienced an open Heaven above his life that mightily affected the entire earth. I believe that his dream revealed a picture of what the unseen realm looks like above our own altars of prayer, intercession, worship, and devotion.

Ancient Paths

The kind of prayer journey we're speaking of is an historical, biblical tradition. It is not a new fad. God is restoring ancient pathways so that His people can become empowered to succeed in the end times. God does fight for us while we're focused in devoted, worshipful prayer. We see it again and again in the Bible and throughout Church history.

While we're on the mountaintop erecting an altar of prayer and worship, God is fighting for us in the trenches. Angelic power is released to move strongholds out of our way and raise up the Kingdom of God in our midst. The Joshuas on the frontlines of ministry are helped, encouraged, strengthened and empowered for success.

Worshiping and praying in God's presence will cause an enduring altar to be built over your life, just as it was with Jacob's life. Your life of prayer and intercessory worship will become a place where angels ascend and descend. Building an altar is a very important spiritual concept, and those who devote their lives to prayer and worship become servants at God's altar and servers at God's table.

> And the twelve summoned the congregation of the disciples and said, "It is not desirable for us to neglect the Word of God in order to serve tables. But select from among you, brethren, seven men of good reputation, full of the Spirit and of wisdom, whom we may put in charge of this task. But we will devote ourselves to prayer, and to the ministry of the word.
>
> —Acts 6:2-4

The apostolic call involves serving at the table of the Lord—to worship and minister unto Him, to sup with Him. This will enable you to go out from that place empowered to feed the saints for the ministry. This ministry at the altar of God and ministry at His table provides the ability for you to become poured-out wine and broken bread for the hungry. Many people will be able to eat at your table because you have eaten at God's table.

You build an altar in prayer as you struggle daily to press through distractions, hindrances, the dross in your own heart, apathy, and much more. As you pray and worship God diligently, you are pressing into His presence. As you experience a greater and greater sense of His presence, the enduring spiritual breakthrough becomes your altar of prayer and worship. Over time it will become increasingly easy to enter His presence, until a day comes when little more than a whisper brings Him near to you or you closer to Him.

One day, you will go to your prayer room to kneel down and pray, and you'll find the Holy Spirit there waiting for you. At that point, you will realize that you've built something tangible in the spiritual realm. You've constructed a spiritual altar with your worshipful prayers.

Now, you'll begin to notice that the spiritual climate has changed dramatically. You may even begin to experience miracles! You've taken territory in the spiritual realm.

The Impact of an Altar

An altar of God's presence is a spiritual reality that is very holy. So holy, in fact, that anything that comes near that altar is sanctified or made holy by its very presence. Jesus speaks about the importance of the altar in Matthew 23:19: "Which is more important, the offering or the altar that sanctifies the offering?" Jesus Himself testifies of the spiritual significance of altar.

You can be sure that Jacob's life was dramatically impacted after he experienced God's altar during his sleep. Your life will be dramatically impacted, too.

Although the sacrifices in the Old Testament were offered by killing animals, ours are of a different kind. At God's altar we raise sacrifices of prayerful praise and worship as priests. This is a vertical relationship with the Lord. We also offer prayers of intercession. This is the act of taking a horizontal relationship with others and their needs to a vertical relationship we have with our Lord Jesus Christ.

Now, here's a powerful revelation: When we are priests at a particular altar, we share in that altar, according to 1 Corinthians 10:18: "Are not those who eat the sacrifices sharers in the altar?" This means that the spiritual blessings and gifts that are alive and flowing from that altar are ours, too. If we are praying at an altar of healing, our own health as well as the health of our families will be released also. If we are priests at an altar where faith is being released to empower people to do great things in God's Kingdom, the same gift of faith will be ours, also. So, you can see that there are great privileges and benefits associated with building a spiritual altar.

Reverence for an Altar

In Malachi, we read about the Israelites getting into great trouble for having the wrong attitudes in connection with the altar of God.

> *"You are presenting defiled food upon My altar. But you say, 'How have we defiled Thee?' In that you say, 'The table of the Lord is to be despised.' But when you present the blind for sacrifice, is it not evil? And when you present the lame and sick, is it not evil. …Oh that there were one among you who would shut the gates, that you might not uselessly kindle fire on My altar! I am not pleased with you," says the Lord of hosts, "nor will I accept an offering from you…. "You also say, 'My, how tiresome it is!' And you disdainfully sniff at it," says the Lord of hosts and you bring what was taken by robbery, and what is lame or sick…."*

—Malachi 1:7-8,10,13

It's so important that we not come before the Lord lightly. We must come reverently, soberly, with attitudes of love and holiness. We must never come for the wrong reasons, for the Bible warns that such sacrifices will not be pleasing to God, to you, and those you are praying for.

When you lift up a sacrifice of worship at a holy altar of prayer, do so with your whole heart. Worship with a heart of genuine gratitude, thanksgiving, respect and love. When you do, the fire of God will touch your altar and great things will happen.

Chapter Seven

WAITING UPON GOD

My soul, wait thou only upon God; for my expectation is from him.

—Psalm 62:5, KJV

For seven days we are completely on God's clock. Our schedules, our agendas, our wants and needs, our plans and expectations are all checked at the door. This time is God's time, and everything we experience is accomplished according to His plan—not ours.

Understanding God's timing is one of the primary keys to going deeper in God. We must understand and believe that He will take us deeper, that He wants us to go deeper with Him, and that it must be accomplished according to His time and plan. We are there merely to wait upon Him.

And so, we wait and watch for Him. We come before Him and wait for Him to show up, to pour out His Spirit upon us and to usher us into a new depth in Him. For it's "not by might nor by power, but by My Spirit says the Lord of hosts." (Zech. 4:6). All is accomplished by Him, and our part is simply to wait before Him and enter into His presence.

Andrew Murray calls this place of waiting the "true place of man."

"These wait all upon thee, that thou mayest give them their meat in due season. That thou givest unto them, they gather; Thou openest thine hand, they are satisfied with good" (Ps. 104:27-28, ASV).

This psalm praises the Creator of all creation and it sums up the whole relationship of creation to its Creator and its continuous dependence upon Him in the one phrase: they all wait upon Thee!" Just as much as it was God's work to create, it is His work to maintain. As little as man could create himself, is he left to provide for himself. The whole creation is ruled by one unalterable law of waiting upon God!

Their word is the simple expression of that for the sake of which also one man was brought into existence, the very groundwork of his constitution. The one object for which God gave life to mankind was that in them He might prove and show forth His wisdom, power, and goodness. He would be, each moment, their life and happiness, and pour forth unto them the riches of His goodness and power. And just as this is the very place and nature of God, to be unceasingly the supplier of every want, so the very place and nature of man is nothing but this—to wait upon God and receive from Him what He alone can give, what He delights to give.[1]

Waiting upon God is a place of spiritual positioning. In other words, during intercession waiting on God places us in a position of utter dependence upon Him. With all of our being we acknowledge that He is God and we are the created.

Although some may consider waiting a completely passive act, it is actually very active. For while we wait we are expectant, and we are full of faith. Our hearts are reaching toward Him, while we maintain a position of being the beloved, the object of His divine affection. We are the receiver, and He, the divine giver. We are the created, and He, the Creator.

Going deeper in God requires that you understand only He can take you deeper, and that He greatly desires to do so. Waiting upon God becomes an acknowledgement of holy trust, of divine rest.

Silence in His Presence

A deep well of God's presence resides in the inner being of every Christian. And in that well of God's Spirit flows a fountain of healing. As we quiet our flesh, that fountain of living water springs up within us, overflowing our souls with the virtue of God. It is through stillness and silence that we tap into those healing springs of God's wonderful Spirit.

Silent prayer before the Lord is not an outward action. This communion is expressed in a deep connection of your heart to God's heart, your spirit to God's Spirit. Silent prayer is active listening—it is communication without words. It is deep prayer that fills the heart with unspeakable joy—a joy that brings divine rest, healing, and refreshment to your soul.

Discovering the Ancient Paths for Ourselves

Because our lives are so busy, how then do we get back to the simplicity that God intended for us? We must get away from it all and take time to be with the Lord, and do as the Scripture commands: "Stand by the ways and see and ask for the ancient paths, where the good way is, and walk in it. And you shall find rest for your souls. But they said, 'We will not walk in it.'"

This passage tells us to understand, and pray and ask God for these ancient paths. *Ancient* means "concealed; the vanishing point; eternal, lasting, of old, perpetual, and secret." Finding them also requires that we walk in them.

Stand, See, Ask, Walk

Scripture tells us to: *stand*, which means to position yourself or put yourself in a position to receive from God. It's a waiting and being still before God. *Stand* means to be willing to take the time.

See means to watch for, look for and expect by faith that God will do and will be what He promised. He is the same yesterday, today, and forever.

Ask means to make a request in prayer for revelation, understanding, and insight into the ancient pathways. These are the spiritual pathways of the saints of old and the timeless understanding of ages past. We ask for this wisdom so that we might understand and know God better today.

Walk means to live and move and have our being in God. Our walk suggests that our lifestyle has its foundation upon the Word of God.

Once we have come into His presence to stand, see and ask, and the truths have been revealed, we then are given an opportunity to walk in them with conviction and consistency. The rest for our souls that is so desperately needed in the chaotic world in which we live will be lived out in our daily lives.

We must see as Daniel saw in his end-time vision of Father God and our Lord Jesus Christ. Daniel had to position himself mentally, emotionally, and physically to stand, see, ask, and walk in the mighty vision he received from God. Daniel 7:9-10 says:

> *I kept looking until thrones were set up, and the Ancient of Days took His seat; His vesture was like white snow, and the hair of His head like pure wool. His throne was ablaze with flames, its wheels were a burning fire. A river of fire was flowing and coming out from before Him; thousands upon thousands were attending Him, and myriads upon myriads were standing before Him; the court sat, and the books were opened.*

As he kept looking, he saw God. In Daniel 7:13, he reveals: "I kept looking in the night visions." His eyes were opened to one of the most complete and wonderful visions of God ever recorded.

The key to receiving this incredible vision was that Daniel had positioned himself to see and experience this revelation of God. He took time to wait and watch. He kept looking until the Ancient of Days Himself showed up to reveal Himself and to provide insight into what He was going to do that would affect the entire world at the end of time. These were spectacular eternal truths that Daniel was privileged to see.

In order to find rest for our souls, we must steal away with Jesus and take time to concentrate on Him alone. We must slow down to do as they did in years gone by. They actually took time to wait upon God, rest, and pray. Men and women in the Scriptures, along with our forefathers and foremothers who were modern day saints, took time to get away with the Lord and to hear His voice and wait upon Him.

During the reign of Louis XIV, Madame Jeanne Guyon wrote about entering into the depths of God through prayer. Her teachings later dramatically influenced the Pentecostal forerunners of our times, including the Moravians, John Wesley, Andrew Murray, Watchman Nee, Hudson Taylor, Jesse Penn-Lewis, and many others. About waiting on God, she said:

> You are now ready to know about another aspect of prayer which I will simply call the prayer of faith and stillness. After you have been meditating in the Word and praying it out to God for some time, you will gradually find how easy it is to come into His presence. You will remember other scriptures with less difficulty. Prayer has become easy, sweet, and delightful. You have now found, dear one, the true way of finding God and that His "name is as ointment poured forth" (Song 1:3).
>
> Now, I want you to pray a little differently. You must now begin to use your faith and courage without being disturbed at the difficulties you may encounter. First, as soon as you come into the presence of God, remain in respectful silence for a little while. Remain there in His divine presence without being troubled about a subject for prayer. Simply enjoy God. …Seek nothing from God during these quiet moments except to love Him and please Him.[2]

What happened after these saints of old waited upon God and watched for Him? They heard profound things waiting in His presence and had profound words to speak to the Body of Christ. They were His trumpeters and His revivalists. I also long to be a revivalist for the Lord and hope that I can be a part of helping to revive God's people.

Revivalist Evan Roberts spoke of how waiting upon God was a constant and expected part of the Azusa Street revival. He wrote to one man seeking revival:

> My dear brother in the faith: Many thanks for your kind letter. I am impressed with your sincerity and honesty of purpose. Congregate the people together who are willing to make a total surrender. Pray and wait. Believe God's promises. Hold daily meeting. May God bless you, is my earnest prayer. Yours in Christ, Evan Roberts.[3]

These powerful revivalists understood the key of waiting upon God in His presence, sometimes for hours and days, simply to hear a word from Him, or to be bathed in the light of His wonderful presence.

I believe that all of us can be revived; and as we are revived, we can revive others. But we must first get away to hear what God has to say. When God speaks directly from Heaven in the quiet moments of silence into a waiting heart, the words He speaks can ignite a flame of revival that will change a nation.

I believe this is one of the sounds that God has given me and I believe He wants to raise up many others who will sound that trumpet of returning to the old paths. Will we listen and hear Him when He calls. Jeremiah 6:17 says, "I set watchmen over you saying, 'Listen to the sound of the trumpet,' but they said, 'We will not listen.'" What will be your own response?

Discovering Ancient Paths for Ourselves

The saints who walked ancient paths were men and women who walked barefoot, in a manner of speaking. They were vulnerable and broken before God, empty of themselves and full of the Holy Ghost. They were people who had no confidence in their flesh, but were real live flesh-and-blood people who were His trumpets. They spoke His words and lived His life. They loved the way that He loved. It is possible for us to live that kind of a life, though we struggle with that concept and wonder if we could. But, if Christ is in us, we can live that life just as the saints of old did. For it is Christ in us, the hope of glory—the glory of ages past, present and future.

I have desired to be like a saint of old. It's not that I want to be old fashioned. I want my life to represent eternal things—the eternal principles of the God of eternity Who never gets old! I want to have the same sensitivity to God that the saints of old had. Slowly, over time, our generation has lowered its standards and not realized it. We've diminished what it means to be a Christian, and our lowered expectations have become the standard. Although acceptable to us, these standards do not please God. Most of us live very far beneath where God has called us to live.

Prospering Through Waiting on God

Our physical prosperity and health are contingent upon the prospering of our souls: "Beloved, I pray that in all respects you may prosper and be in good health just as your soul prospers" (3 John 2). Sometimes our material prosperity doesn't come until our soul prospers and we learn to be at home in the heavenly realm, enjoying it more than we enjoy the earth. Then because we are enjoying the heavenly realm our earthly prosperity does not become a hindrance to us.

The Bible teaches us to "rest in the Lord and wait patiently for Him. Do not fret because of him who prospers in his way, because of the man who carries out wicked schemes. Cease from anger, and forsake wrath; do not fret, it leads only to evildoing. For evildoers will be cut off, but those who wait for the Lord, they will inherit the land" (Ps. 37:7-9).

Waiting upon the Lord brings our souls into a place of rest. All the fretting, worrying and planning in the world will not bring God's prosperity and purposes into our lives, but resting and waiting upon God will.

While we wait upon God, resting in His presence, something happens in our souls. We are being set free from striving and fretting. We are coming to a place of rest. The 23rd Psalm promises that the Lord will lead us beside quiet waters and we will find rest for our souls. It's in the quiet moments of waiting upon God that this rest is imparted.

We leave that place of prayer with a new tranquility, with a new peace about us. Our thoughts are not so frantic. We have a new perspective on life and our situations. We have a deeper sense of trust that God will work out all our situations.

Strength Through Waiting

Great strength is imparted as we wait patiently before the Lord. Isaiah 30:15 (NKJV) says, "In quiet and confidence shall be your strength." We come into a place where we begin to realize in the deepest places of our inner man that God really is with us, that He really is on our side, He really is helping us and leading us. We let go a little and let God take control a little more each time we wait patiently before Him.

As I wait in that rest before God, the strength of the Holy Spirit is released to mount up inside my spirit man and my own strength is brought to a place of rest. "But they that wait upon the Lord shall renew their strength; they shall mount up with wings as eagles; they shall run, and not be weary; and they shall walk, and not faint" (Isa. 40:31, KJV). In other words, they hope in the Lord. In *Strong's Concordance, wait upon* means "to bind together; to collect; to gather together; to look patiently; to tarry or wait."

Oswald Chambers said, "My soul, be silent unto God. Rouse your soul out of its drowsiness to consider God. Fix your attention on God, on the great themes of His redemption and His holiness, on the great and glorious outlines of His character, be silent to Him there; then be as busy as you like in the ordinary affairs of life. Be like the Lord Jesus; when He was sound asleep in the fishing boat He knew that His Father would waken Him when He wanted Him. This is a marvelous picture of confidence in God."[4]

Fighting Our Battles While We Wait

Much of waiting before Him is a posture that quietly trusts that while we are looking toward God, He is looking at our enemies. He is looking out for our interests. He is looking toward our concerns. Exodus 14:13 commands us: "Stand by and see the salvation of the Lord." We have but one concern—to look into His wonderful face. When we do so, He will bring prosperity to our souls, deliverance to our bodies, and wrath upon our enemies.

Who or what are your enemies? We all have them. Are your enemies habits and fears? Are they forces of lack and poverty? Are your enemies walls and hurdles erected against your progress and success? Stop looking at your enemies. Turn your gaze instead and look into His face. When you do, He promises to silence the accuser and stay the hand of those who hate you.

Read the promise of Psalm 37:32-40:

The wicked spies upon the righteous, and seeks to kill him. The Lord will not leave him in his hand, or let him be condemned when he is judged. Wait for the Lord, and keep His way, and He will exalt you to inherit the land. When the wicked are cut off, you will see it. I have seen a violent wicked man spreading himself like a luxuriant tree in its native soil. Then he passed away, and lo, he was no more; I sought for him, but he could not be found. Mark the blameless man, and behold the upright; for the man of peace will have prosperity. But transgressors will be altogether destroyed; the posterity of the wicked will be cut off. But the salvation of the righteous is from the Lord; He is their strength in time of trouble. And the Lord helps them and delivers them. He delivers them from the wicked and saves them because they take refuge in Him.

Inheriting the Land

Those who learn to wait upon God and upon His strength will inherit their promised land, whatever that promised land happens to be in their lives. Waiting upon the Lord is so very important: "Wait for the Lord and keep His way; and He will exalt you to inherit the land" (Ps. 37:3-4).

While you wait upon God, faith and strength rises within you; but that is not all that is happening. Beyond your prayer room, God is moving angelic forces into place to work on your behalf. He is moving events and circumstances so that while you wait patiently in faith, He is working toward the day when you will receive all He has promised. While you rest in Him, He works for you. That's a great exchange!

Isn't that something? Let's go back to verses 3-4 in Psalm 37: "Trust in the Lord, and do good; dwell in the land and cultivate faithfulness. Delight yourself in the Lord; and He will give you the desires of your heart."

We are encouraged to cultivate faithfulness. *Cultivate* means "to feed securely or feed on his faithfulness." Cultivating takes time and patience. A farmer plants seeds and patiently waits for them to grow. He doesn't dig up the seeds he has planted to see if they're growing under the ground. He cultivates his land. We must feed on His faithfulness. We need to walk and work spiritually like the farmer. After the farmer has done all he knows to do in preparing the ground, planting the seed and watering it, he waits patiently for the fruit of his labor to spring up from the ground.

Evildoers will be cut off, but those who wait for the Lord will inherit the land. He takes care of all that concerns us as we wait for Him, as our souls rest before Him and trust Him for all His benefits and promises. Our occupation or our preoccupation should be with God. In His own timing, He will cut off those who do wickedly. "Yet in a little while and the wicked man will be no more; and you will look carefully for his place, and he will not be there. But the humble will inherit the land, and will delight themselves in abundant prosperity" (Ps. 37:10-11).

Much Has Been Accomplished

I waited patiently for the Lord; and He inclined to me and heard my cry.

—Psalm 40:1

As the presence of God gently lifts, we realize that we've done little more than wait in His wonderful, lovely presence. Yet, we leave the place of prayer with a deep sense of knowing that He has heard us, His ear is toward us. We have looked to Him and waited upon Him, and He is bending low with His ear turned in our direction, carefully listening to the cry of our hearts.

Our souls are very peaceful, very quiet, very rested from deep within. Like David, we say, "I have quieted my soul, like a weaned child rests against its mother" (Ps. 131:2). Our hearts are quieted before God. Yet, somehow we know that much awaits us in the stillness of our waiting, expectant prayer watch. We are experiencing the living reality of God's precious Word: "For from of old they have not heard nor perceived by ear, neither has the eye seen a God besides Thee, Who acts in behalf of the one who waits for Him" (Isa. 64:4).

As our prayer time ends, I feel that God is saying a word to us. Much has been accomplished in the heavenly realm. A lot of battles have been won while we've taken the time to come up here and wait upon the Lord.

⸘ ENDNOTES ⸘

1. Andrew Murray; *Waiting On God*; Whitaker House; New Kensington, Pennsylvania; 1981; p. 19-20.

2. Madame Guyon; ed. Donna C. Arthur; *Experiencing God through Prayer*; Whitaker House; Pittsburgh, Pennsylvania; 1984; pp. 23-24.

3. Frank Bartleman with Vinson Synan; *Azusa Street*; Bridge Publishing; South Plainfield, New Jersey; 1980; p. 15.

4. Oswald Chambers; *Still Higher for His Highest;* Zondervan; Grand Rapids, Michigan; 1971; p.67.

Chapter Eight

OCEAN WAVES —
THERE IS A FOUNTAIN

Deep calls to deep at the sound of Thy waterfalls; all Thy breakers and Thy waves have rolled over me. The Lord will command His lovingkindness in the daytime; and His song will be with me in the night, a prayer to the God of my life.

—Psalm 42:7-8

Here on the California coast, I'm continuing my spiritual pilgrimage at a beautiful beach home called Ocean Waves. I've spent hours watching the waves and reflecting upon my wonderful Bridegroom and what I have experienced in the depths of the precious Holy Spirit.

This particular beach house sits on a cliff that juts out into the ocean. As I've been sitting here on the edge of land, I've been considering how God is calling me and the entire Body of Christ to come out to the edge—to come out on the bluff and be willing to take some major risks.

Seeing the ocean from this perspective is breathtaking. This panoramic view is absolutely spectacular. It causes me to consider how each one of us often has such a small view of God, what He has for us, and what He wants for us.

Nevertheless, God wants to give us a big view—a big view of Himself and a big view of all He has for us. But it will take us stepping to the edge, willing to lay down our fear and our intimidation, to lay aside every weight that hinders us and every encumbrance that holds us back, especially those weights and hindrances we carry deep inside.

If you think about it very honestly, who is the one that hinders you from God's very best? It's probably you. We limit ourselves more often than anyone else sets limitations upon us, and far too often we limit ourselves because we are unable or unwilling to deal with those things that we hold deeply within. We tend to think in such small ways, but God wants us to think big—and to especially think big of Him.

This beautiful Pacific view, this breathtaking panoramic view makes me want to think about the greatness and grandness of God. Oh, my goodness! It's endless what God has for you and me. We're His people, and He is a great, wonderful, loving, powerful God. His purposes for us are vast.

As I look out from the edge of the cliff at this wonderful, beautiful Pacific Ocean, I can't see where it ends. It's endless—just as God's love is endless. God speaks to my heart, "This is what My love is all about. It's a bottomless well and an expansive ocean of love, and it's all for you, My people."

Oh, to know as Paul prayed, the height and depth of the love that is in Christ Jesus (see Eph. 3:18). The revelation of the fountain of His love is the greatest revelation we will ever experience, and it's endless. There's always more! Once we experience that fountain of His love, we are cleansed and healed and restored in a way that nothing else can match.

His Love is Like a Fountain

We will never see the end of His fountain of love. Too often we limit His love. We say that He cannot really love "me" that much. But, His love for you and me is like this expansive Pacific view.

He is saying to you, "I have so much love for you My son and My daughter. You will never see the end of it. It's so deep it cannot be measured. It's so wide that you'll never be able to take it all in." He wants you to experience the depths of His love—wave after wave after wave of it. As David cries out in Psalm 42:7-8:

Deep calls to deep at the sound of Thy waterfalls; all Thy breakers and Thy waves have rolled over me. The Lord will command His lovingkindness in the daytime; and His song will be with me in the night, a prayer to the God of my life.

David understood that in the depths of Jesus Christ is love that washes over a soul in waves. Wave after wave of endless love crashes over our sin-sick, thirsty souls as we touch the ocean of His endless, expansive love through prayer. In this depth, healing and cleansing take place in a way that's permanent, lasting, and powerful.

God wants us to experience the fullness of His love, the depths of it, the crashing waves of it. He wants us to experience wave after wave of His sweet presence and holy, unspeakable love.

I understand now why I needed to travel in my pilgrimage to a place called Ocean Waves. He wanted to underscore the revelation of His love in the beauty of these endlessly crashing waves as I've watched the tide go in and out.

Stepping Out to the Edge

There are so many trials and so many tribulations that come against our lives discouraging us from coming to the edge for a better view of what God has for us. You know, if I had not come to this edge, I would never have experienced this beauty, this spectacular view, this glorious panoramic of God's creation.

I could have stayed away from this edge for fear of falling or tripping and tumbling down. If I had not exercised my faith and laid down my fears, taken the risk and challenge by coming to the edge, I would have missed the glory of the Lord manifested. What about you? What fears are keeping you from coming to the edge and experiencing more of God? What fears are holding you back from going deeper in God?

What the Depths Are All About

Here at this place where the land juts out into the mighty ocean, God is providing a living picture of what His depths are all about. Entering the depths of God requires coming to the edge—being challenged to go beyond what has been familiar and comfortable. I stand here on the edge, but my heart is reaching up toward God.

Sometimes the Lord will take us into a place where we are hidden, much like the tree house-like cabin in the woods that I visited surrounded by tall redwoods. It was a place that makes you feel hidden from everything, totally surrounded and very secure. Some places in God feel like that—sheltered, hidden, safe, and secure. And at other times, He takes us out on a cliff, and He makes us stand out there all alone, to take some risks and be challenged to go beyond where we've ever been. At such times it seems there is no secure place to be found.

Beyond Your Limitations

I am reminded of what the Lord spoke to me some years ago. He said, "I am not limited by your limitations." Here, looking into the mighty ocean, God is saying, "Take the limits off Me. Do you want all that I have for you? It is more than you can ever fathom. It is more that you could ever imagine."

The Body of Christ has stopped believing God for great and mighty things. There is so much that He wants to give us. Yet, we struggle each day with the same limitations just trying to get by. The Lord wants to heal our soul and help us fulfill our calling, destiny, and purposes here on earth. But first we must take the risk to step out!

We've grown so accustomed to the dull ache of life that comes from being unhealed and not cleansed in the deepest parts of ourselves, that we press forward each day with the same lack of abundant life. Some of us have waited so long to be healed deep inside that we've forgotten that we ever believed we could be healed. Others of us have ignored the ache for so long that we don't believe that healing is really possible or necessary—at least for us.

Finding genuine healing in God may require coming to the edge of uncertainty. But, if we keep our eyes on the ocean of Christ's mighty love for us, we'll be cleansed by the waves of His presence.

Cleansed Superficially

Jeremiah 6:16 speaks of the ancient past and things that have been lost, such as stealing away to spend time with Jesus: "Thus says the Lord, 'Stand by the ways and see and ask for the ancient paths, where the good way is, and walk in it...but they said, 'We will not walk in it.'"

Historically the Church has understood that walking in wholeness requires a genuine, private devotional life of time spent in earnest seeking and obtaining a touch of God's presence upon our daily lives. The old hymns were written from this ancient path of understanding, and many, such as "Steal Away to Jesus" and "In the Garden" were new songs that arose from the hearts of those who knew these well-worn ways of God.

Lacking this "ancient path" we have sometimes experienced a gospel of quick fixes, which unfortunately doesn't provide the deep cleansing and healing paid for at the Cross and thus prevents us from fulfilling our calling and destiny:

"And they have healed the brokenness of My people superficially, saying, 'Peace, peace,' but there is no peace. "Were they ashamed because of the abomination they have done? They were not even ashamed at all; they did not even know how to blush. Therefore they shall fall among those who fall; at the time that I punish them, they shall be cast down," says the Lord.

Thus says the Lord, "Stand by the ways and see and ask for the ancient paths, where the good way is, and walk in it; and you shall find rest for your souls."

—Jeremiah 6:14-16

Here God tells His people that they were being healed superficially because they had lost something they had once had. Something ancient and eternal, something from the past had been stolen from them. We are experiencing this same loss in the day in which we live. We are being healed superficially. We are attempting to put Band Aids on our problems, hurts, and wounds, but we're not receiving the genuine, deep cleansing from the fountain of God that is available to us as our birthright and that will help us to be more productive and effective in this life to the glory of our Lord.

As a people, we are not whole and we are not healed—not really. We attempt to bring healing through the latest fads. We run here for these three steps, and when we're not satisfied we run somewhere else for the next quick fix. But, all the while, we're living with the same dull aches of sin, wounds, and spiritual diseases that have plagued us all of our lives.

God wants to set our sights higher, to raise the standard and show us that we can do it because we have Him. Then we will be able to walk those ways of the past that will bring to this new day something that is eternal. When we reclaim that which we've lost we'll have something wholesome and healthy to give to people who are dying spiritually and emotionally, both Christians and non-Christians alike.

We need to go back and recapture what we've lost. We need to rediscover the ancient pathways, the paths that our ancestors walked to become mighty men and women of God. We must rediscover the ways that are not so much old and ancient as they are eternal principles that never get old or die. God is calling us back to the simplicity of truly knowing Him, for there the "ancient path" of His presence is a fountain of life, a fountain whose waves will wash away the sin and sickness that resides deep inside our souls.

Blow the Trumpet

In Jeremiah 6:17 notice God's advice on behalf of those who are being healed superficially. He tells His people: "I set watchmen over you…" We who are people of prayer, we who are prophetic intercessors and prayer warriors, are appointed by God to sound a trumpet of truth warning God's people.

It's because we have been with Him that we cannot help but to hear His words and speak them to His people. His warnings come easily to us because we have been in His presence, we have cultivated a relationship with Him. We have set ourselves apart just as Moses did when he walked up the mountain and received the Ten Commandments written by the finger of God onto tablets of stone.

In that place of communion and prayer, God speaks words of hope, words of grace, and He builds within us faith to believe Him. What we fix our eyes upon is what leads and guides us. When we fix our focus upon Jesus Christ, He becomes all that we see. His sweet words become what we hear. His heart becomes our own in that secret place of prayer, and that is what heals us. When we are people who live in the depths of God's presence, we become an extension of Him on the earth. We become His people in deed.

Healed Superficially

In Jeremiah 7:4, God's people are warned not to trust in lies. "Do not trust in deceptive words, saying, 'This is the temple of the Lord, the temple of the Lord, the temple of the Lord.'" God was warning not to trust those who say everything is all right; this is God's temple, and He will bless us no matter what we do.

As I said previously, God's people are supposed to be His trumpets, but sometimes those trumpets are not heralding the right message, a pure message to a lost generation. Too often God's people are being healed superficially by being told that everything is all right. What you're doing is okay. Where you are is fine with God. Yet, His people remain uncleansed and unhealed. They continue to steal, murder, commit adultery, swear falsely, and offer sacrifices to other gods.

> *"Will you steal, murder, and commit adultery, and swear falsely, and offer sacrifices to Baal, and walk after other gods that you have not known, then come and stand before Me in this house, which is called by My name, and say, 'We are delivered!'—that you may do all these abominations?"*
>
> —Jeremiah 7:9-10

The most interesting part is that these people do not seem to realize what they're doing. God must send watchmen to help them open their eyes to the true state they are in.

Clean Hands and a Pure Heart

The Lord reveals to us that we must go back and revisit some things. There are places along the way where we've left some things behind. We've lost some things. We've pushed ahead before the time, or we've received some wounds that were never properly treated. Our hearts have sustained some damage; we've held onto some grudges, and we've never let go of some injuries. There are uncleansed places deep inside of us that we've never allowed the Lord to open up and cleanse. All of these things eventually affect our motives for continuing to worship and follow the Savior.

We must take the necessary time to revisit the old paths of God and some old paths of our own lives to make sure that we're lifting up clean hands and pure hearts. Let's look at the powerful promise of God when we do so: "Then

I will make to cease from the cities of Judah and from the streets of Jerusalem the voice of joy and the voice of gladness, the voice of the bridegroom and the voice of the bride, for the land will become a ruin" (Jer. 7:34).

When we are disobedient to the Lord and put other things before Him, when we give place, time, and energy to many things that are not from Him, we will become dull. We will find ourselves disobeying Him and falling into sin because we no longer hear His voice.

The joy of our salvation is diminished, and we lose our gladness. We no longer hear the Bridegroom. No longer are we swept up in the rapture of bridal love.

A Fountain That Cleanses From Hindrances

He's not speaking, but even if He were to speak we wouldn't be able to hear because we do not take time to get away and listen, nor do we take time to rid ourselves of the things that hinder us from hearing. When we make it a habit to get away and hear God our ears become increasingly tuned in to Him, which dramatically impacts everything about us.

You are the salt of the earth; but if the salt has become tasteless, how will it be made salty again. It is good for nothing anymore, except to be thrown out and trampled underfoot by men. You are the light of the world. A city set on a hill cannot be hidden. Nor do men light a lamp, and put it under the peck measure, but on the lampstand, and it gives light to all who are in the house.

Let your light shine before men in such a way that they may see your good works, and glorify your Father who is in heaven. Do not think that I came to abolish the Law or the Prophets. I did not come to abolish, but to fulfill. For truly I say to you, until heaven and earth pass away, not the smallest letter or stroke shall pass away from the Law, until all is accomplished. Whoever then annuls one of the least of these commandments and

so teachers others, shall be called least in the kingdom of heaven; but who-
ever keeps and teaches them, he shall be called great in the kingdom of
God. For I say to you, that unless your righteousness surpasses that of the
scribes and Pharisees, you shall not enter the kingdom of heaven.

—Matthew 5:13-20

When people wound you and hurt you and do all kinds of terrible things against you, do you find it is easier to focus on the hurt than the solution? The Bible provides the answer to hurts that hinder our ability to love people and ultimately to love God and ourselves.

Relationships and the Fountain of God's Presence

God's standards are very high. In order to live according to those standards we must live our lives in His wonderful presence, drinking in moral and emotional strength from His fountain of delights. Matthew 5:21-22 warns us: "You have heard that the ancients were told, 'You shall not commit murder,' and 'Whoever commits murder shall be liable to the court.' But I say to you that everyone who is angry with his brother shall be guilty before the court; and whoever shall say to his brother, 'Raca,' shall be guilty before the supreme court; and whoever shall say, 'You fool,' shall be guilty enough to go into the fiery hell."

The Bible suggests that relationships with others are vitally important in respect to our own ability to enter into the depths of God's presence. How you treat your brother matters much to God. As a matter of fact, if you bring an offering to the altar and remember that your brother has ought against you, you must go to him first and make it right.

If therefore, you are presenting your offering at the altar and there remem-
ber that your brother has something against you, leave your offering there

before the altar and go your way. First be reconciled to your brother and then come and present your offering.

—Matthew 5:23-24

This is a major way that prayer keeps our relationships pure and healthy. As you come into your place of prayer, you may discover that God wants you to deal with unhealed, uncleansed relationships. Perhaps you were angry with someone before you knelt down to pray. God may remind you of your need to go and make that right before you enter into the depths of prayer. Be quick to obey, for there will be a reward for your quick obedience from the Father.

Nothing Less Than Love

What does God expect? How should you act toward everyone, even sinners? God expects no less than love.

And if anyone wants to sue you, and take your shirt, let him have your coat also. And whoever shall force you to go one mile, go with him two. Give to him who asks of you and do not turn away from him who wants to borrow from you. You have heard that it was said, "You shall love your neighbor and hate your enemy."

But I say to you, love your enemies, and pray for those who persecute you in order that you may be sons of your Father who is in heaven; for he causes His sun to rise on the evil and the good, and sends rain on the righteous and the unrighteous. For if you love those who love you, what reward have you? Do not even the tax gatherers do the same? And if you greet your brothers only, what do you do more than others? Do not even the Gentiles do the same? Therefore you are to be perfect as your heavenly Father is perfect.

—Matthew 5:40-48

Nothing less than love will do in God's eyes. If you have treated anyone poorly and remember it in prayer, do everything you can to make that right. If you've offended, sinned, cheated, or harmed another in any way, let that cleansing fountain get your heart right and keep your heart right before God.

A Cleansing Fountain for Healing and Cleansing of Relationships

When I go before the Lord and pray, I pour out my heart. I cry. I complain. I do whatever I need to do with God, and He lets me hear myself. He feeds back to me what I said and the attitude of my heart, so that I can hear any attitudes or motives that might not be pleasing to God. That's when I realize there are some things that I might need to do differently.

I make these corrections in my own heart before God's throne. When the correction is made, I then try to practice it and be obedient. To do so requires His grace, which He always supplies. I may need to go back and walk in love with those who have hurt and wounded me. Perhaps their motives and intentions continue to be the same. It doesn't matter, for I have made a commitment to God at the altar of prayer. He will help me to walk in love, no matter how difficult.

Sometimes coming away for a time of prayer is a way of removing yourself temporarily from a difficult interpersonal relationship in order to gain some perspective—God's perspective. How easy it is to get caught up in the petty jealousies and emotional battles of daily life. With so many bullets flying at us, it becomes very difficult to get the bird's eye view—God's view.

Nothing is healthier than stepping out of the fray of a difficult situation for a few moments of peace and prayer. You may even discover that you are doing or saying things that are inflaming the situation. You also may receive God's strategy for overcoming even the most difficult interpersonal problems.

His presence is a fountain of cleansing that will spill beyond the borders of your prayer life and pour peace and grace into those who touch your life.

When we find ourselves in difficult relationships and difficult circumstances with others, we find ourselves rehearsing over and over again those things that are hurtful to us. This person said this. That person said that. Why was this done in this particular way? Our thoughts and questions can get overwhelming.

But in that quiet place of prayer, when the lover of our soul begins to pour into our hearts the oil from His fountain, we leave those thoughts and begin to praise Him. As we quietly worship Him, He assures us that He will make it right. He will help. He is on our side. He is all we need.

The Lord is a heavenly treasure. Yet, too many of us leave the treasure of His delightful, healing, soothing presence unexplored. There in the quiet place of prayer, He will become your Wonderful Counselor, your Prince of Peace. These are not mere names. They are who He is, and who He will be for you and your present need, no matter how pressing.

As you enter that cleansing fountain, lay down the sin, faults, hurt, anger, bitterness, and disappointment. Rehearse the things that are hurting you. Pray from your heart and not your intellect. Sometimes it helps to shout. Sometimes it's good to cry. Emotions can get locked up in us, controlling us, consuming us, and eating us up, yet we don't realize it. But when we come before Him and spend intimate times, our spirits seem to groan in His presence and such emotions get taken care of. It's a release.

Receive His forgiveness for your sins and offenses, and then let Him release you. Start praising Him and worshiping Him in earnest. You will discover, maybe for the first time, what it means to take your burdens to the Cross and leave them there.

Repentance and Cleansing

People tend to confuse repentance with confession, but they are two different things. After we acknowledge our shortcomings, sin, frustration or whatever, then we confess it to God.

The next step after confession is repentance. Repentance is an act of turning away from sin, literally taking action and starting to do something very specific and direct. What we start to do is often the opposite of what we've been doing. If we hated, we will now love. If we've slandered behind someone's back, we will now be honest and truthful about what we've said directly to that person's face.

When we repent, we literally go beyond confession and are then converted or saved from whatever that particular thing was that we were doing. We no longer do it. So often when we say, "I repent!" "I repent!" we really aren't repenting at all. We're merely confessing our sin. Repentance is something that we actually see in our actions, that we literally do after we have confessed. We take action to do the opposite.

Repentance occurs when we replace an evil feeling with a holy one, or an evil action with a good one. Repentance is a process that takes a little time to show that it's work has been accomplished. It's a complicated matter, and I believe we have often trivialized it. We have joined in prayer for individuals and even for the corporate Body, asking God to pour out His Spirit for confession and cleansing. We have considered it repentance when people were truly sorry for their sins. However, that is simply confession. Repentance is always revealed in action.

The fruit of true repentance results in a change of behavior. Simply experiencing a cleansing time in prayer over sinful behaviors and actions is not all that is required to be loosed from sin. After getting up from prayer, changes must be done earnestly and sincerely. The Scriptures speak of a sorrow that accompanies repentance. Yet, much of the repentance we see today seems to have little genuine sorrow connected with it. True repentance is a deep and sincere matter of the heart.

Some of our prayer for national cleansing and revival is much like this. We cry out to God to come by His Spirit and make a difference in the lives of people so that they might live righteous, holy lives. The Holy Spirit will respond to those prayers and come in power to give those individuals an opportunity to repent and change. Conviction falls and people respond. They cry out to God for cleansing because they recognize how awful their sin is in God's sight. Even so, true repentance, turning from sin, sometimes does not follow. We must remember that individuals have a choice.

One of the reasons that we tend to take emotional experiences lightly is because there have been so many times when such emotional encounters with God do not transform lives. We weep at the altar but get up and leave just the same. Our lives are not transformed. We haven't experienced the ancient path principle of the fear of God, which is essential for a transformed life.

Remember that when God cleanses you at His fountain, you have the responsibility of obedience in order for genuine and lasting transformation to take place.

Covered In the Fountain of His Love

Early this morning I was awakened at about 3 a.m. with an opportunity to look out at the sparkling water under the luminescence of a brightly moon-lit sky. It was low tide, and in the place of crashing, foamy water were rocks and seaweed.

I thought, *My goodness, It's amazing. I didn't realize that so much was there, and so much was on the sand.* Just as the tide comes in and covers many things, so there are things in us that need to be hidden and covered in God. When the ocean of God's presence washes over our lives it covers up so much—the rocks and the seaweed inside of us. All of the rough and ugly places inside of us are hidden under His mighty love.

God by His Holy Spirit has been washing wave after wave after wave over my being, covering up some things that need to be covered up, because some of it has been quite ugly and no one else really needs to see it.

And it's really interesting that when the tide was out at its lowest ebb and it was darker, that's when the ugly parts could really be seen. When the tide came in as it became daylight, those parts were covered.

You know, no one but God really, truly sees and understands all that I've gone through—all that's hidden deep inside, covered under the glorious presence of His awesome love. I can share those hidden, dark places with Him, and He can reveal them to me.

In the darkness of the nighttime hours, God can reveal the dark, hard, rough places hidden inside my soul. There is no one here but me during those quiet hours, and He is so kind and gracious that I can receive the truth that He reveals.

As we come into His presence needing to be cleansed of deep sins that no one knows about, He washes us in the fountain of His presence with waves of wonderful mercy, sweet anointing, and cleansing water from the ocean of His love. In the morning we are covered with His presence, and no one else has to see what God has covered.

During those private times God allows us to pray when we're not fearful or afraid. In fact what is so wonderful about our God is that He doesn't always show us everything about ourselves. He doesn't always show us every picture of the really rugged and ugly part of ourselves. He just lets us see enough to bring us to His cleansing fountain.

Yet, He sees it all, and that's all right because He understands it all. He is kind enough to let us see just enough so that we can give it to Him. He lets us understand just enough of the ugliness so that we can confess and repent. I'm pretty sure that if we could see it all exactly the way He is able to see it, we would not be able to bear it.

As it is, what He has allowed us to see we don't like. We'd make changes if we could. But He is so gracious and kind that He lets us see just enough so that we'll allow Him to come in and wash it away with the waves of His very own presence. That is what He is doing with my life and I believe that is what He wants to do with your life as well.

Chapter Nine

HE RESTORES MY SOUL

The Lord is my shepherd; I shall not want. He maketh me to lie down in green pastures: he leadeth me beside still waters. He restoreth my soul.

—Psalm 23:1-3, KJV

Your own pilgrim's journey up a mountain of prayer will be filled with delights and surprises. On one of my prayer pilgrimages, I was prompted by the Holy Spirit to take along a friend whose name I'll call Amanda.

We arrived at our cottage situated deep in the beautiful Californian sequoia forest. I came to draw near to God and pray; Amanda came for many reasons. Amanda later shared with me that although she had worked as a full-time children's minister for years, she had not experienced the touch of God upon her life in prayer since childhood.

Amanda had been wounded deeply as a children's ministry worker at a large regional television station. When I met her at a women's conference she was defeated and worn out. After she shared a little about her story, I realized that it was vitally important for Amanda to steal away to Jesus, to get away from it all and into the presence of God where she could be restored by Him. There are times when nothing else will do but to get into the depths of His wonderful, holy presence where restoration and healing freely flow.

Because Amanda's experience in God's presence so well represents the subject of this chapter, I decided to allow her to share her story of restoration and healing. Although what she shares is very dramatic, you may find yourself identifying with many of the events and circumstances she has undergone.

Amanda experienced a fresh encounter with the Holy Spirit in that little cottage nestled among those great big trees and hidden under the magnificent, fragrant umbrella of green summer leaves. There in His presence, she was deeply transformed, healed, and restored, and will never be the same.

"I feel as though He has taken me to a place that I have never been before," said Amanda. "I feel like I'm being peeled like an onion, with layer upon layer coming off me. I also feel love as I have never felt love before."

I asked Amanda what the love felt like.

She replied, "It's warm, cozy, thick, and it's reassuring. His presence has been non-stop since I arrived here at this prayer cottage. Not only can I sense His presence during prayer—like earlier today when we were in the other room and His presence was so strong—but His presence was very strong when I got up this morning."

I asked Amanda why she thought His presence was so strong upon her throughout this time of prayer.

"He wants me to really know, to finally really know that someone loves me, and not just anyone, but God Himself loves me. His presence feels like warm, thick honey wrapping me up in love."

Amanda felt the need to share with me how she came to this place of pressing into the depths of God in order to find more of Him, which for Amanda included having God restore her of deep and significant life-long wounds, which were blocking her path and hindering her personal spiritual progress.

Before Amanda started reaching out for more of God, He started drawing her into the depths of His wonderful presence. "Draw me, we will run after thee," (Song 1:4, KJV). We never desire to journey deeper into God without

His first calling us there from His throne. "Deep calls to deep," said the psalmist (see Ps. 42:7).

"When the Lord started dealing with me about prayer, I started getting up and going over to the prayer room at the television station at 6 a.m.," said Amanda. "I had received a prophetic word several years earlier in which the Lord said to me, 'You know a lot *about* prayer, but I want to teach you to pray.' He said this to me two different times."

Amanda began to experience deep, inner longing, which she calls an "ache" for God.

The Cry of a Hungry Heart

"The Holy Spirit helped me to pray for my ministry and for my city. He gave me a real burden for my city, but I still had an ache for God that I didn't really understand. I just wanted more of Him. I came to the point at which I would go to the prayer room in the mornings just to cry out for more of Him. I would push those prayer requests out before me and I would say, *Lord, You know what's on these papers, but God, I need You.* That really became the cry of my heart. I just needed Him. I didn't even care to know more things about the Lord; I just wanted Him.

"If I couldn't have Him then I didn't want anything. I wanted Him. I cried out to Him. I said, *Lord, I need help, I need help. Holy Spirit, You're the teacher; You've got to help me.* This went on for a long time. My prayer wasn't answered right away. The desire for Him kept getting greater and deeper."

Amanda's heart cry for more of God continued for five years. She had been accustomed to teaching and preaching the Word of God; she had spiritual gifts that were operating in her life, but her walk lacked power because she didn't know Him intimately.

Amanda said, "I didn't want just God's ability. I don't want His ability now. I want Him. I needed His presence in my life in a way that I had not experienced. That was what my heart was crying out for. When I suggested that I didn't have God, what I meant was I wasn't experiencing the reality of waking up in the morning and sensing the friendship of His presence."

Amanda woke up every morning and got a cup of coffee and sat down to read her Bible. She was actually feeding her mind with the Word of God instead of feeding her spirit man with the intimacy that comes with His wonderful presence.

"I was learning more information about the Lord so that I could teach about Him, but I wasn't reading the Word of God to find Him, and He was the one I wanted. I had done the other for so long that I didn't even know how to look for Him in the Bible," she said.

Amanda had been caring for her mother, but a year into this whole process her mother died and she found herself alone with much more time on her hands. Her stepfather passed away the very next year.

"Once she died," said Amanda, "I felt like my life took a turn and all of a sudden I was going in a new direction. I didn't have anyone else to worry about, or to do for or to see after. And the hunger in my heart for God just kept growing stronger."

"When your parents die, no matter how old you are, you feel like an orphan, especially when you don't have any other family," Amanda said. The only other relative Amanda has is her sister. This relationship had been deeply strained after Amanda's sister's 20-year-old husband raped Amanda when she was 12 years old.

"A couple of years ago she talked to me on the phone about what had happened years before. You know what she said? She said, '…the day you had sex with my husband.' They didn't stay married long after that, but they were together then. I had always thought that he raped me, but in her mind it was consensual."

We had never talked about it before this particular day. "She said, 'Well, you know, the day you had sex with my husband…I just want you to know that you don't have to worry about it because it's under the blood.'"

As a Nine-Year-Old Child

Amanda shared that this was not the only violation she had experienced as a child. When she was just nine years old, she had endured another ruinous encounter.

"I grew up in a Christian home. I can never remember not going to church as a child. Both of my parents seemed very dedicated to serving the Lord. They both taught Sunday school and we were involved in some type of church activity all the time. I always believed in God as a child," said Amanda.

"But the year I turned nine, my life took some major turns. My dad started seeing another woman, and that summer both Mom and Dad thought it would be good to let me go and spend the summer up in the mountains on a horse ranch with a couple whom they had known for years. They also were Christians, and he had actually been a pastor.

"I was excited to go, and so a week after school was out I left for the ranch. About three days after I got there my little world turned upside down. Both of them worked during the day and I was left to do whatever I pleased. He drove a truck and could come home when his schedule permitted. That third day I was there, he decided to come home just shortly after his wife had gone to work. It was still very early in the morning, and he came upstairs to my bedroom. I thought something bad had happened and I started to get up. He was there for an entirely different reason. He raped me. When he left, I just laid there. I wasn't exactly sure what had happened.

"He had signed me up to take English riding lessons every Monday evening and on the way home, it was his custom to park the car and horse trailer down some dark road and take more sexual privileges with me. I would beg his wife to come with us, which she did occasionally, but not regularly.

"Come the next year, dad was continuing his affair and my life at home was very bad. My mom was broken in spirit and very close to having a nervous breakdown. They both felt that sending me back to the ranch for the summer was a provision from the Lord for me, I'm sure. I told myself now that I was older, maybe he wouldn't try what he had before. Maybe his wife didn't have to work anymore.

"I avoided him as much as possible. I told him that I wouldn't be taking riding lessons in the evenings. But he seemed to always find a place and a time when no one was around. That summer I was ten.

"My dad eventually moved out of the house. I never told Dad or Mom what had happened to me. I knew she couldn't have taken it, and I didn't want him to know. In my mind, he was doing the same thing to someone else that had been done to me. The person that he had left my mom for was just eight years older than me. I guess I thought that he would have felt that what had happened to me was okay. It sounds ridiculous, but not for a child's thinking.

"I never saw that couple again and never spoke of these things for years. I pushed it all to the back of my mind and did a fairly good job in trying to forget it. Then several years later, I was visiting my sister's home. She had gone to the store and I had lain down on the couch to take a nap. I don't remember her husband coming home; I only remember being awakened by him. What he did to me didn't take long, and, thankfully, never happened again. He left again before she came home. I didn't know until several years ago that she even knew. I was far too embarrassed to tell anyone. I guess he wasn't."

These sexual violations were the blocks or hindrances that Amanda needed to be healed from. Amanda's ability to be intimate was violently stolen from her. That sexual intimacy was merely one aspect of true intimacy, which involves the total person, body, mind, emotions and spirit. Sexual violation created a deep wound that shut down Amanda's ability to explore the places in her heart that involve spiritual and emotional intimacy. Today, Amanda remains unmarried. More unfortunate, however, has been her lifelong inability to walk in spiritual intimacy with her Lord.

Falling Apart

After Amanda's mother died and her role as caretaker ended, her sense of security crumbled and she admits her life fell apart.

"My world fell apart. Everything that I was comfortable with, felt at home with, all the grace that I had, to do the jobs that I did—everything began to change," said Amanda. "I had been fairly good at everything, but now, I couldn't do anything anymore, and I didn't have the desire to do anything. I couldn't preach, teach, work in the office. I wasn't able to be with people, counsel with people or minister to them. I felt as though the person I had been for all of those years disappeared, and I didn't know where she went. The me who was left was a stranger to me. I felt dead inside. I was a Spirit-filled Christian, a minister in full-time ministry, and I felt dead inside. I didn't have any life to give."

The person who had left was a person who never was, someone who had gone through all the acts and assignments of another person. Eventually, that individual who really wasn't Amanda ran out of strength and came crashing down. What was left was the real Amanda who had been hidden and buried under this competent image for years.

"I didn't recognize her. She doesn't know what to do. She doesn't know what to say and doesn't know how to act. She feels very insecure, very out of place...lost. And the other Amanda always had an answer and always knew what to do to get the job done."

For decades Amanda had been the one in charge. She was always in control, always knew just what to do. She even had left the country on her own and ministered to children in the Third World with wonderful results. Still, she did not experience intimacy with God, but ministered out of her gifts and knowledge.

"I was not intimate with the Lord, even then," said Amanda. "God was a good friend who would show up when I needed help. That's a lot different than intimacy. I called on Him only when I needed help.

"But it wasn't intimate, in that I didn't worship Him, I didn't love Him, spending time telling Him that I loved Him, and I never gave Him any time to love me. I would get up and I would pray but it was formal. It wasn't like He was the lover of my soul. It wasn't like He was the one I longed for. It wasn't that at all. My devotion was done out of habit."

In truth, God was actually missing and longing for more of a personal encounter with Amanda. But, sadly, she didn't realize that there was more of God than what she had already experienced.

Amanda did not have a manifestation of His presence to touch her in the deep spiritual places of her heart, and the deep emotional places of her heart were not being met, especially those areas that had been affected by the painful experiences she had as a child. The deep places where she had been wounded and broken as a child were never ministered to.

Out of Your Belly Shall Flow Rivers

Just recently, Amanda's heart cry before the throne of God began producing dramatic results. It began as she was listening to a worship CD in her home and softly singing to the Lord in prayer.

"I was listening to a CD and worshiping when I felt something deep in the pit of my stomach. I felt the presence of God deep within me—I physically felt something."

Before long, Amanda was lost in sweet, wonderful worship to God.

"I was lost in worship, and then I became aware of my circumstances again and I stopped worshiping and was surprised at what I had felt. I wondered what it was. It was a deep feeling of warmth and excitement within me. Since I had already been filled with the Holy Spirit and had spoken in tongues for years, my question was, What was that? I knew it was God, but I was experiencing Him in a way that I had not experienced Him prior to that moment."

Amanda felt God begin to stir something down in the depths of her belly.

"Once I had the assurance that it was Him and that it was something that I was in much need of, I almost felt like one of the little babies I saw in Romania who were stuck in a crib with no one to come and hold them or touch them or love them. They become emotionally deformed and scarred in their mental growth because of being untouched. That is what I felt like, and that small touch from God just made me know how much I needed God's touch."

"No one around me knew I was that way, but I was in a bad condition. Every day only made me more aware of my need, of my lack, of my true condition."

Amanda hadn't even realized that she could receive more from the Lord than she had already experienced. She really didn't have a clue that there was so much more to be experienced in the depths of God's presence.

In the last day, that great day of the feast, Jesus stood and cried, saying, "If any man thirst, let him come unto Me, and drink. He that believeth on Me, as the scripture hath said, out of his belly shall flow rivers of living water."

—John 7:37-38, KJV

Amanda began to receive a fresh flow of those rivers of living water. It began with a sort of "flutter." It was a trickle of life flowing up from the depths of her innermost being.

Over the next several weeks, Amanda and I started going off together to seek God in earnest. Through a process of a few weeks of waiting upon God and then coming back to Him again, spending time seeking Him, worshipping Him and waiting upon His presence, a manifestation of God's presence began to break through. A river of living water, as a gusher, started flowing into and through her soul.

A Breakthrough Comes

"One morning you were encouraging me to just begin to speak aloud to the Lord what was really within me. At first you suggested that we start with singing a song of praise. I believe it was 'How Great Thou Art.'

"I wouldn't sing. I felt as though I couldn't sing. It was at the point that I realized how bound up I was inside. Then you told me to praise and worship God and tell Him how much I loved Him. But, you know, I didn't even want to do that. I was used to doing those things in front of a church full of people. Yet, there that morning, the words were stuck somewhere inside of me and would not come out.

"I knew that if I was serious about getting something more from God that I was going to have to break through my hesitation and do it now. So, I started praising God, although it was very faint at first. I had to force myself as if the words were locked up inside of me and wouldn't come out.

"I pressed in, even though I felt embarrassed and backwards in my approach. Nevertheless, I kept it up and eventually I began to feel a little freedom in my worship and in my crying out to God. As I continued to cry out for the Lord, I found myself telling Him of my deep desire for Him, how I longed for Him.

"Then I began to break, and it was like one little gate had been opened—that was the beginning. His presence came and just settled over me, and all I could do was cry and shake.

"John 6:56 speaks of Him abiding in me, because of His blood. The 15th chapter of John speaks of Him abiding within me. I had not experienced Him in this fullness before. I actually felt the love and the freeing power of the Holy Spirit in a new way."

Healing Streams Flow From God's Throne

In Revelation 22:1-3 we are told that healing streams flow from the throne of God.

And he showed me a river of the water of life, clear as crystal, coming from the throne of God and of the Lamb, in the middle of its street. And on either side of the river was the tree of life, bearing twelve kinds of fruit, yielding its fruit every month; and the leaves of the tree were for the healing of the nations. And there shall no longer be any curse; and the throne of God and of the Lamb shall be in it, and His bondservants shall serve Him.

This scripture means that His wonderful, lovely presence heals us. If we are seeking healing, we need to seek Jesus. He Himself is healing. In His presence is where we will be healed. As Amanda experienced the depths of God's presence, the broken, unhealed emotions hidden since childhood began to be healed.

"My emotions were being healed, and I was beginning to remember His sweet abiding presence. It was wonderful, and it just made me want more of the Lord. I found that I wanted to stay in a place of His presence. Later, I would wake up thinking of Him and go to sleep thinking about Him. During the day, I began to let myself long for Him and seek him. When I could get into a place of prayer, He began to come in powerful ways.

"His presence began to touch me over and over again, shaking me from the inside out. Healing began to take place within me, spiritual, emotional, and even physical. His presence was changing every part of my life."

He Restores My Soul

In that secret place of God's wonderful healing presence, God began dealing with the wounds of Amanda's past, healing the wounded, broken, and bruised places in her soul from very, very deep within. Psalm 23:3 says, "He restoreth my soul."

"In His presence, I felt as if a load was lifted off of me. I walked out from underneath a load that I did not have to carry anymore. I had never shared some of the details from my past with anyone before. It was a closed, lock door. During one of our times in prayer, the Spirit of the Lord came so sweetly and in such a loving and yet powerful way. He began to expose those areas within me that were still in need of healing.

"I knew I was in a safe place, and I just allowed Him to minister new life to me. You prayed for me, and I experienced a true deliverance from the hurts and wounds of my past. We must 'confess your sins one to another and pray for one another that you may be healed. The effective prayer of a righteous man can accomplish much' (Jas. 5:16). I had never confessed some of those things before. I knew I had been forgiven, but what I didn't understand was that I still needed to be healed. I had just closed the door and allowed those things to stay in me. I had not opened the door to God's healing power and grace," said Amanda.

When God started to come and manifest His presence and stir those waters down in the depths of Amanda's belly, she started to have a release, a healing. That release came as the living water inside washed her, bringing genuine, lasting deliverance, which is nothing more than healing.

Removing the Stones

In the story of Isaac, we learn that the enemy had come and filled up the well Isaac had dug with stones (see Gen. 26). He had to re-dig that well, which is a picture of what happens in our hearts.

Events, circumstances, traumas, and attacks to our hearts can be likened to Isaac's enemies. Stones are hurled at us and block up the wells to our hearts and the living water deep within becomes impossible to reach. Sometimes the healing process is through the removal of things that were there, which is why some people use the term *deliverance.* There is a need for healing, but before healing can be accomplished something must be removed so that the healing process can flow.

Amanda said, "That's the way I saw myself. I felt as if I was damned up; and when the Holy Spirit began to flow through me, at first it was only a trickle. Even the way I allowed the Holy Spirit to use me at church and in my ministry was very controlled. I didn't yield to anything that might put me out of control. I made sure I was in control all the time. I didn't allow the Holy Spirit to have His way, therefore, the Holy Spirit didn't flow through me very much. I was so damned up that what I experienced with the Holy Spirit seemed normal, even though it was just a trickle. I had been comfortable with it being that way for years. When the Holy Spirit began to remove those rocks, I began to get set free; those rocks were a lot of hurt and wounds from the past."

Restoring Intimacy—A Healing Process

Amanda had been violated intimately, and God came and touched her intimately to deal with those painful issues of her past.

After this initial encounter in the depths of Christ, Amanda went on to experience a succession of encounters and breakthroughs as He dealt with one layer after another layer of wounding and restoration.

"I was so broken within myself, but then the Holy Spirit would come and bring healing. I enjoyed the healing presence of the Holy Spirit. This seems to be an ongoing process—being broken, and experiencing healing. He was peeling away the hurt just like an onion. I would say, *Oh thank You Father. That is finally gone.* And then He would show me something else."

The Bread of Heaven

John 6:41-58 says,

*The Jews therefore were grumbling about Him, because He said, "I am the
bread that came down out of heaven." And they were saying, "Is not this
Jesus, the son of Joseph, whose father and mother we know? How does He
now say, 'I have come down out of heaven.' …Jesus answered and said to
them, "Do not grumble among yourselves. No one can come to Me, unless
the Father who sent Me draws him; and I will raise him up on the last
day. It is written in the prophets, 'And they shall all be taught of God.'
Everyone who has heard and learned from the Father, comes to Me.*

*"Not that any man has seen the Father, except the One who is from
God; He has seen the Father. Truly, truly, I say to you, he who believes has
eternal life. I am the bread of life. Your fathers ate the manna in the
wilderness, and they died. This is the bread which comes down out of
heaven, so that one may eat of it and not die. I am the living bread that
came down out of heaven; if any one eats of this bread, he shall live forever; and the bread also which I shall give for the life of the world is my
flesh." The Jews therefore began to argue with one another, saying, "How
can this man give us His flesh to eat?"*

*Jesus therefore said to them, "Truly, truly, I say to you, unless you eat
the flesh of the Son of Man and drink His blood, you have no life in yourselves. He who eats My flesh and drinks My blood had eternal life, and I
will raise him up on the last day. For My flesh is true food, and My blood
is true drink. He who eats My flesh and drinks My blood abides in Me,
and I in him. As the living Father sent Me, and I live because of the
Father, so he who eats Me, he also shall live because of Me. This is the
bread which came down out of heaven; not as the fathers ate, and died,
he who eats this bread shall live forever."*

Amanda experienced this passage firsthand. Jesus became her spiritual
drink and her food. He became a part of her entire being. Prayerful communion with the Father through Jesus Christ brought a healing, restoring flow into
her soul that has continued its work to this day.

Come to His Healing Presence

If you have hurts and wounds, whether they are physical, mental, emotional, or spiritual, God can and will restore you. In His presence there is fullness of joy, according to Psalm 16:11. Amanda found the deep healing and restoration that her soul needed for many years. She found those things in the depths of Jesus Christ.

Chapter Ten

CROSSING OVER

I know a man in Christ who fourteen years ago—whether in the body I do not know, or out of the body I do not know, God knows—such a man was caught up to the third heaven.

—2 Corinthians 12:2

I don't know what time it was—about 3 or 4 o'clock in the morning, maybe earlier. It was dark all around me, and I was completely alone in my bedroom at the Crow's Nest where we began this prayer journey, which I've tried to record for you within the pages of this book. There in the quiet stillness of that mountain cottage His wonderful presence woke me from my sleep. A glorious warmth filled my being, and that precious presence became increasingly tangible, until I began to realize that the Lord Himself was standing there in my room with me.

It was at that point that I crossed over...

I was completely bathed, immersed in His wonderful love. It was an indescribable experience. I felt as if every part of my being was being loved by Him—every part of me was being taken over by Him. Just as the eagles that nested in the mountain right below our window must feel, I felt as if every part of me was free. He had taken complete control.

You may be wondering what I mean by "crossing over." Where did I go? Well, crossing over means that you've crossed the threshold, you've gone through the veil of this life over into the one that awaits you with Him. It's a place of union with God.

Few modern preachers speak of the possibility of finding union with God experientially while here on earth. In fact, some discourage even talking about it. Nevertheless, it is a well-worn ancient pathway that many of our grandfathers and grandmothers have told us about.

Madame Guyon, in her book, *Union With God*, said, "What are we seeing here? The inner man has become partaker of an unutterable, inexpressible communion with the Trinity. The Father of Spirits imparts His spiritual fertility and makes the inner man to be one with the Lord Himself. Just as the believer's spirit has always been one with the divine spirit ever since his conversion, now his inner man is united with the Lord by means of having been transformed…It is here that unutterable secrets are revealed, not by illumination, which is momentary, but revealed in God Himself. (It is in God that all secrets are hidden.)"[1]

Crossing over involves entering the inner chamber of God. It felt as though I had received a new sense of freedom and as if I had been enraptured in His love. I felt totally free, and at the same time, I also felt very enclosed in a secret place of His wonderful presence.

I felt as though I was flying with eagles, soaring, and I was also entering into a place of timelessness. It was like a taste of eternity.

Total Acceptance

Do you know what it's like to feel loved all over? We already are accepted in the Beloved, crossing over involves entering into a tangible sense of total acceptance by God, feeling that God is so happy with you, so delighted with you, in fact, that your inner man can truly rest in the glowing warmth of that eternal love. This has nothing to do with performance or what you've accomplished in your life.

It is a mutual feeling and precious fellowship with Him that occurs in the deep presence of God. I was being loved by Him, but at the same time my love for Him was greatly increased. The intensity of that mutual love just kept getting larger and broader. Paul prayed for the Ephesians: "That He would grant you, according to the riches of His glory, to be strengthened with power through His Spirit in the inner man; so that Christ may dwell in your hearts through faith; and that you, being rooted and grounded in love, may be able to comprehend with all the saints what is the breadth and length and height and depth, and to know the love of Christ which surpasses knowledge, that you may be filled up to all the fullness of God" (Eph. 3:16-19).

In the Song of Solomon, the bride tells her heavenly groom, "I am my beloved's and He is mine. His banner over me is love" (Song 2:4). That secret place is a chamber of deep, intense, and mutual divine love. It is an experience of love like you've never imagined, and it is different and unique for each individual. It's pure, holy, tender, and completely intimate. Loving Him in that secret chamber will satisfy your deepest needs and greatest longings. This holy love is so pure that it made me feel totally pure and completely clean.

Do you know what was interesting? I didn't feel my own sense of weakness. As a matter of fact, my focus wasn't on myself at all. My heart and mind were not focused on any of my own shortcomings. I felt so free and liberated, and my own sense of self together with all of my shortcomings seemed very insignificant and unimportant in His great presence. I was so focused on the Lord and His beauty that I wasn't even thinking about myself. My whole focus was wrapped up in Him. It was as if I lost my sense of self, and all that I could see was His wonderful, lovely face.

I didn't feel sin. I didn't feel weakness. I had no sense of my own ongoing concerns. I didn't feel my own inadequacies, my own insecurities. In the depths of that wonderful presence such things don't exist. Actually, the truth is I knew I was there, but I felt as if I wasn't. All that seemed to exist was Him. All that existed was the love of God; just the divine, holy embrace, and being engulfed—lost—in His wonderful, sweet love. It was total abandonment, oneness.

Perfect Love

Perfect love casts out our fear:

There is no fear in love; but perfect love casts out fear, because fear involves punishment, and the one who fears is not perfected in love…we love because He first loved us.

—1 John 4:18-19

I was experiencing the perfect love of God, which releases and delivers from feelings of fear. Not only from fear, but also from the intimidation of the enemy that causes us to think about ourselves. Intimidation is a sense of fear that makes us believe we're not good enough to come into God's presence or that only others more special and significant to God are worthy of such visitations. Our Lord desires to visit His people and fellowship with them in special ways that are appropriate for them.

In that depth of God's presence, such matters of fear and intimidation cease to exist. For those moments, it felt that such thoughts had never existed in my heart and mind. That's what was so wonderful—it's like it never was. It made me think that how the Lord removes our sin as far as the east is from the west.

For as high as the heavens are above the earth, so great is His lovingkindness toward those who fear Him. As far as the east is from the west, so far has He removed our transgression from us.

—Psalm 103:11-12

When He forgives our sin, He literally removes it from us. In other words, it's impossible to see it or even remember it anymore. And that's how I felt there in His sweet presence. I felt as if I was pure and holy, just as He is pure and holy. In Him, there truly is no remembrance or residue of sin or uncleanness. It is one thing to know this intellectually, but it is another to know it in such manifested certainty.

Lost in God

I was lost in His holiness, lost in His presence, lost in who He is. One moment I felt like a child, the next moment I felt like a bride, and the next moment like a mature believer.

Such transitions flow instantly from moment to moment. At one moment you're a baby and the next you're a shy bride who has just been kissed. Seconds later, you're a mature woman who has spent years in relationship with her partner. It was all of that, all at one time, because you're touching the timelessness of the heavenly realm.

You talk about soaring! My goodness, this overwhelming experience is far above that level because it's higher still, and there is always more. You are crossing over into His inner chambers and into Him. You experience timelessness, spacelessness, and you are released from the world and all its cares. You are released from yourself and your own self-consciousness. It's sheer enjoyment—sheer delight! It's ecstasy. You become enmeshed with God. You become one with Him in the most real and literal, tangible sense.

Moments of Release

I believe that God allows us these special times so that we can rise above all the responsibilities, demands, and pressures of daily life. God gives us a spiritual respite from our daily grind. Through these treasured, precious moments, we are released from the weight of all our cares. We are free from all of our responsibilities—they no longer shackle us. They become in the most practical sense God's burden instead of ours.

Please don't misunderstand me. I'm not suggesting that we become irresponsible. However, in these moments of God's presence all our worldly weights are lifted. We leave that presence with a genuine knowledge that we do not carry the weights and encumbrances of life alone. We have One who is always with us, whether or not we are presently feeling and experiencing Him in the depths of His presence. He truly is our burden bearer, and the yoke of our responsibilities becomes lighter and easier. Our minds are cleared and our spirits cleansed when all our burdens are lifted by God.

How often I've walked with friends and acquaintances who are weary and tired in body and mind and feel that they cannot get even a moment of rest or refreshing. There is a place in God where we can go to find sweet relief. Most Christians live for years carrying the weight of their lives, work, and ministries without ever experiencing this sense of spiritual relief in His presence.

The Scriptures say that in Heaven there is no more sorrow, pain, or sickness.

For this reason, they are before the throne of God; and they serve Him day and night in His temple; and He who sits on the throne shall spread His tabernacle over them. They shall hunger no more, neither thirst anymore; neither shall the sun beat down on them, nor any heat; for the Lamb in the center of the throne shall be their shepherd, and shall guide them to springs of the water of life; and God shall wipe every tear from their eyes.

—Revelation 7:15-17

In those moments of crossing over that's what I felt. I was completely free of all the world's stress, pain, tension—all of it. It was wonderfully refreshing and completely healing.

Such moments are a glimpse of glory, a foretaste of the eternal treasure that awaits us beyond the veil of this life. In those holy moments, my heart was raptured, swept up into His loving, wonderful presence, consumed in His sweet, tender love. If you need to be relieved of the heavy burden of weight and care of your life, come to Him for His refreshing drink. He will carry you upon His wings far above every care.

Refresh Me With Apples

The Bible speaks of this heavenly refreshing that takes place in the depths of God's presence in the Song of Solomon. Let's look.

Like an apple tree among the trees of the forest, so is my beloved among the young men. In his shade I took great delight and sat down, and his fruit was sweet to my taste. He has brought me to his banquet hall, and his banner over me is love. Sustain me with raisin cakes, refresh me with apples, because I am lovesick. Let his left hand be under my head and his right hand embrace me.

—Song of Solomon 2:3-6

This passage says "in His shade I took delight" and "His banner over me is love." This is exactly what happened to me when I crossed over. I became completely overshadowed by His presence. It was as if I was consumed in Him, and I ceased to exist. All I felt was love—sweet, precious, wonderful, supernaturally divine love. It was a love that poured into every atom of my entire being, filling me, strengthening me, delighting me, energizing me. His love covered me completely.

The Shulamite, or the bride of the Song of Solomon, says that she took "great delight" in His shade. There is so much delight there, supernatural delight, a heavenly joy that thrills the soul beyond what words can describe. I completely relate to the Scripture: "He has brought me to His banquet hall," because that's exactly what happened. I was drinking His wine, eating of His delights, thrilling in the shade of His presence. And, oh, that fruit was so sweet to my taste!

There is a refreshing in that presence that cannot be described, an energizing and cleansing of mind, soul, and spirit. "Sustain me with raisin cakes, refresh me with apples." These are fruits of His presence that bring great comfort.

In His wonderful presence you will be comforted. You may wonder, *Why would I need to be comforted?* Have you ever wondered why the Holy Spirit is often called the Comforter? You and I and the Amandas of the world need to be comforted quite often by God. The hurts that lie deep within, the aloneness we experience as we walk this earth—all of these things require that our souls and spirits be comforted in order to be strengthened, healed, and filled with joy and love.

In addition, since the 9/11 disaster we have experienced terror on every side. The pressure of world events continues to increase, and attempting to maintain a normal lifestyle has grown increasingly difficult. The Bible warns about the time we're approaching. "And by smooth words he will turn to godlessness those who act wickedly toward the covenant, but the people who know their God will display strength and take action" (Dan. 11:32).

Even in the toughest times, those of us who press closer into God will find the strength and courage to make a difference. No matter what happens, the Lord will always be there to bring us comfort and peace in the midst of every storm.

A Lovesick Bride

The Shulamite asks her bridegroom to refresh her because she is "lovesick." What does this mean? Some consider that "lovesick" is a state of an expectant bride who is so filled with love that she cannot eat or drink or carry on her daily activities for longing after the one she loves. This state is described in this passage, for the Shulamite is singing a bridal song of deep longing for her beloved.

We might consider that this bride needs love desperately, so desperately, in fact, that she is aching with the pang of desire. She is sick because her need for His love is so deep and her desire so strong.

Yet, that is not the only meaning here. *Lovesick* also can speak of "having so much love that a person is carried away by it." She who experiences him is so full of love that she can do little else but bask in the state of ecstasy that his love produces. The lovesick Bride of Christ will gain an ability through this intimate communion to rise up above all fear and every difficult circumstance to do great things for God and for the world.

Both states of lovesickness happen to the one whose gaze falls upon the lovely face of our divine Bridegroom. There have been times in which I was so full of love that I truly couldn't take anymore. I felt that I would burst if I received one more ounce of it.

Conversely, at other times the ache of spiritual desire has been so strong and deep in my inner being that I felt completely distracted from everything but the need to cry out to Him. It's at such times that He becomes our food. With longings so deep, we cannot eat or sleep except that He might come and breathe upon our waiting, expectant hearts and touch us with the fire of His love.

Love's Embrace

Song of Solomon 2:6 says, "Let his left hand be under my head and his right hand embrace me." That's what happened to me in God's presence as I crossed over from this present realm to the divine realm. I felt the embrace of the heavenly Bridegroom, and every part of me was bathed in His wonderful love. I felt as though I was in my physical body, but at the same time I was not. The apostle Paul speaks of this state in 2 Corinthians 12:2. He said, "I know a man in Christ who fourteen years ago—whether in the body I do not know, or out of the body I do not know, God knows—such a man was caught up to the third heaven."

I was also in the spirit, free from fleshly restraints. In that place of supernatural, divine love, I felt pure acceptance, and total, complete, transcendent love.

This was a time of empowerment and equipment for living in this present hour of time. The Lord wants to empower and equip you, too. According to Acts 17:6 (KJV): "…these that have turned the world upside down are come hither also." Those who cross over become spiritually empowered to turn the world upside down.

You've Crossed Over

In the quiet and stillness of the night, I heard a voice say over and over, "You've crossed over. You've crossed over the threshold."

There are times in God when you are in His presence and you are being blessed by Him and encouraged by Him, but you continue to be aware of the world around you and your various concerns in life. All the while He is carrying you and sustaining you during your daily walk with Him. We are in the world but not of it. (See John 15:19.) In this blessed state, we do our work and keep our hearts and minds upon Him. We cast our burdens upon Him and go about our lives and are successful in our spiritual walk.

Yet, there are times when even that state is not good enough. There are times when He wants to take you far beyond what you've ever experienced. These are blessed moments of heavenly delight. In such moments, the world no longer exists. You've been swept up in the Spirit. You've crossed over from the natural to the divine realm.

Sustaining Moments

In such moments, all that seems to exist is God. These moments are not something that you will experience all the time. They are special, chosen, rare treasures that change the way we see our lives forever.

Afterward, you are changed. You feel different, totally refreshed, strengthened. You carry something special with you back into the daily grind of life. You are never again the same.

I've experienced many crossings over where I felt something new had happened and I had gone over to the other side. I believe that sometimes these experiences occur at a spiritual crossroads in life and ministry, or after being wounded or feeling weary. Sometimes they happen when we need healing of soul, mind, spirit, or even body, or when God is preparing us to enter into a new season of ministry.

It doesn't really matter where you are, how many years you've been walking with God, or whether or not you've been a spiritual giant. You need a fresh touch from God regardless of where you happen to be, and you need a touch that is more than just a touch. You need a transforming, transcending experience that will change and cleanse you in a way that nothing else can.

Heaven's Treasure

Be careful not to seek an experience, or to seek having the same experience described by another individual. Always seek Jesus. Seek Him for Himself alone.

When I crossed over I was seeking nothing less than the Lord Jesus, my Savior, my Lord, my God, my Master. I was seeking just to get close to Him. I was hungry for Him, hungry for His presence. There is absolutely nothing wrong with wanting to experience more of His presence. You want Him, and because of that you ultimately experience Him in ways that might have been unimaginable to you just seconds prior. All you have to do is ask Him… "Ask, and it shall be given to you; seek, and you shall find; knock, and it shall be opened to you" (Matt. 7:7).

Know that there is always so much more, more than you've ever known, more than you've ever experienced. Heaven is filled with an eternity of secret delights—all of which are your inheritance in Him. God has hidden treasures waiting for you, and they will be yours for nothing more than simply asking.

✃ ENDNOTE ✃

1. Madame Guyon; *Union with God*; The Seed Sowers; Sargent, Georgia; 1999; copyright by Gene Edwards; p. 48.

To Contact Rev. Pat Chen and for more information
on FLMI, books, CD's and other resources.

REV. PAT CHEN

HEADQUARTERS:
First Love Ministries Int'l Prayer Center
P.O. Box 1977
San Ramon, CA 94583-6977
Phone: 925-244-9600
Fax: 925-244-9604

E-mail: flmi@earthlink.net

Website: www.firstlovepray.net

CAPITOL HILL DIVISION
The Secret Place
Prayer Room Ministry
Armor Bearers
Prayer Shield and Consultation Services

FLMI
P.O. Box 77238
Washington, DC 20013-7238

Additional copies of this book and other
book titles from DESTINY IMAGE are
available at your local bookstore.

For a bookstore near you, call 1-800-722-6774

Send a request for a catalog to:

Destiny Image® Publishers, Inc.
P.O. Box 310
Shippensburg, PA 17257-0310

*"Speaking to the Purposes of God for This
Generation and for the Generations to Come"*

**For a complete list of our titles,
visit us at www.destinyimage.com**